GENERATION X APP[...]

Top 20 Keys to Effective Leadership

By Curtis L. Odom, Ed.D.

Book◆nol◆o◆gy

n. delivering useable information and knowledge
that adds value to people's lives

A NONFICTION IMPRINT FROM ADDUCENT

Adducent, Inc.

www.Adducent.Co

__Titles Distributed In__
North America
United Kingdom
Western Europe
South America
Australia

GENERATION X APPROVED

Top 20 Keys to Effective Leadership

By Curtis L. Odom, Ed.D.

Generation X Approved

Top 20 Keys to Effective Leadership

By Curtis L. Odom, Ed.D.

ISBN 978-1-9375922-8-8 (hardback)
ISBN 978-1-9375922-9-5 (paperback)

Published by Adducent (under its Booknology imprint) in the United States of America -- Jacksonville, Florida
www.Adducent.Co

TABLE OF CONTENTS

DEDICATION

To my beautiful wife and best friend for life, Nelia – Your supportive fingerprints are on my every success. I cannot imagine this world without you to share it with, or my life without you to love. All I do, I do only for you!

To my lovely daughter and best giggle buddy, Alyssa – I hope that this book will remind you one day, long after I am gone, that your Dad took the greatest joys of his life from moments spent looking at the world through your smiling eyes. I love you!

To Strive, To Seek, To Find, and Not To Yield – Tennyson

ACKNOWLEDGMENTS

I would like to express my deepest appreciation for the unwavering support of my editor, publisher, mentor, and friend, Dennis who continues to create an environment in which I was able to explore without boundaries the continued practice of the craft that is being a published author. His advice and counsel, our shared offbeat sense of humor, and similar perspective on life and liberty as a Navy veteran is a continued match for my style. Thank you, Dennis for your partnership, mentoring, and coaching to always be true to self while living and writing with the Navy core values of Honor, Courage, and Commitment.

To my mother, Hilda, thank you for all of your love and support. I am grateful for your wisdom and guidance through my formative years. Your love is truly are a blessing in my life as I always felt your hand on my shoulder through the darkest nights of life as both a boy and a young man. Thanks Mom for everything.

Thanks to my brother-in-law, Hillard for instilling in me the value of education and the importance of not being satisfied with anything less than my best. As the male role model in my personal life, I continue to aspire to follow the example you have set. Your work ethic, creativity, and keen eye for all that is possible dared me to achieve. Your prophetic words to me long ago sound in my ear as my mantra when the toughest of life and career obstacles present themselves... "Short term inconvenience for long-term gain." Brown Dawg, you are my hero!

To my sister, Betty; my mother-in-law, Lucia; my father-in-law, Afonso; my sister-in-law, Allison, and my sister-in-law's husband, Jim. Thank each of you for all of your love, encouragement, patience and support. You guys are the greatest cheerleading squad one could ever hope to have on the sidelines.

Your faith and confidence in my success are the warm winds in my open sails, pushing me along on an open sea of endless possibilities.

INTRODUCTION

"Leaders aren't born they are made. And they are made just like anything else, through hard work. And that's the price we'll have to pay to achieve that goal, or any goal."

—Vince Lombardi

My First Leader (Mentor)

For most of us our parents are the first examples of leadership we witness in life. And our father or mother (often both) become mentors at perhaps the most important level and degree that we experience until adulthood (and even then it may be equaled but not exceeded).

For me, my father has always been "Pop" and although I lost him when I was four years old, his imprint will never fade. I am the man that I am today in part because of him. I often reflect on my short time with him, and in that brief span I learned much. To work hard, treat people with respect and dignity, and most importantly, that life is more important than work.

My Pop was a hardworking man. But he knew that taking his son for a walk to get the newspaper, to the park or just to sit and watch TV together, was more important than doing other things. From reflecting on that, I realized it's okay to step off the fast track to be there for family. The standard he set through what he did, not just what he said, gave me what I use for a benchmark as a man, husband, father and business professional. I deconstructed how I felt about my Pop and what I learned in our too short time together to form the way I live and the core values that establish who I am as a person. His leadership (and that's what it was at its most basic level) gave me a set of ideals that are still with me today.

As you read this book, take the time to reflect on your core values and what's important to you in life because that is important in order to take away the very best from what you're about to read. Take the time to review how you handle different situations and different people (those you work and interact with in your business or profession and at the personal level, too). Check to see if you held strong to your values. Are you consistent? Are you fair? It's so easy to get caught up and strung out (and along) in the day-to-day chaos of modern life, but it's so important that you take some time every day for yourself. Reflect, think, relax or exercise... whatever it may be... but do something for yourself. Turn off your email and take a few moments to just be who you are (or the improved version of who you can become) and be who would make someone, perhaps your first mentor, proud.

Who Owns Your Career

Why is what I said in the preceding section important? Because today, more than ever, it's important to know who you are in order to establish your value—and that's not to be construed as coming up with an egotistical overestimate—you have to realistically know your self-worth. Here's why:

You may think you own your career, but the reality is you do not. Not fully anyway. Not if you work in Corporate America. The reality is that the truth lies somewhere in between. You can manage your career, and you can work hard to network, build your contacts, scout for new opportunities, but there are decisions that get made every day outside of your control.

You are subject to the whims of others. You are subject to variables outside of your influence.

People are making subjective decisions about you that you may not be able to change. They have perceptions about you. True or not, they are the reality from which people begin to view you and talk about you.

This is all a part of human nature. But you don't have to feel, "it is what it is..." You can combat some of it, though navigating the unknowns and the uncontrolled or a professional career is not easy. It takes a good deal of effort; a great deal of politicking and a ton of work.

There are steps you can take. You can learn to navigate the politics and how to be more astute. You can start to influence others by being vigilant. It does not happen overnight; it takes time. And as Gen Xers it's difficult to be patient enough for the right opportunity. But it's even worse for the Millennials behind us (they are even more antsy than we are). They want to lead today and will, if they are able to, push us aside or under.

This is partly the challenge we face. We can easily get stuck in the middle if we don't start actively taking control of our career opportunities. We may not own our careers fully, but we can direct them. We have options to make the right decisions. To actively pursue what we want we need to balance eagerness with patience. We need to be smart about the opportunities that we pursue and to be aggressive.

The time for us to lead in Corporate America is quickly approaching. You may not own all the decisions that are about to be made, but if you want to be unstuck, now is the time to learn how to influence them.

The Challenge (And Taking a Mulligan)

The Challenge

A good deal of my professional career has been spent building leadership programs across various levels in diverse organization. And, I have seen a lot of good and a lot of bad leaders come through those programs. I have watched as people successfully transitioned to the next level and beyond and sadly I have seen people flame out and fail to move on; not reaching what they expected or aspired to.

What I observed and noted for most that failed is they were not ready psychologically to lead. It was not that they lacked the mental capability or the talent; psychologically they weren't willing to make the sacrifices needed for leadership. They were too hung up on how they used to work and were not prepared to give that up and shift their beliefs, their time and their focus to step up. In the end, it came back to bite them. Each person was considered a superstar; labeled as high potential before entering the programs. Each one was a good worker; smart and fully capable of making the successful transition. But, for each one, there was some impediment in their mental make-up that prevented them from committing to the right concessions so they could get to that higher level.

Some were making the transition into the first level manager role and they could release the need to micromanage in order to delegate to their employees. They wanted to remain the Star, so they could swoop in to "save the day" when something went wrong. In reality being that way only alienated their people and emphasized to their bosses their limitations or inability to truly "manage"... i.e. "lead" people.

Others were making the move into a general manager role. These were the true definition of Superstars. One in particular had moved quickly through his organization, was assigned to complex initiatives throughout his career and was rising steadily. He seemed to be on a fast-track making all of the right connections. But when it came time to manage across functions, he could not let go of his marketing roots. The people in operations and finance found it hard working for him. He was not able to build a culture that would support cross-functional cooperation. In the end, those he should be leading all bickered and the environment degenerated into ugly office politics that played out to the extent he was sent on his way.

It is tough being a leader in an organization of any size or complexity. It takes a great deal of effort to move up in an organization. Where most people fail is not on the talent side (many have the skills, and if there is a gap, it is usually pretty easy to get them up to speed). The challenge is getting them to think differently. Mental adjustment can be a difficult process (and for some it's an impossible one), but it is that mental flexibility that often dictates who succeeds and who fails.

Taking a Leadership Mulligan

If you're a golfer or are familiar with golf you probably know what a mulligan is. If you're at my level of play you definitely know what one is. It's a "do-over"... take another swing at the ball (with the hope you get a better result).

If you had a mulligan available to you in your business life, what would you use it on? Would you change anything important? Would you change your profession, your industry, your work habits or your ethics? I've often thought about what I would "do over."

I don't know that I would change anything in particular, though. There were some mistakes and bumps along the way, but I've grown from them and see them as an opportunity to learn. I love what I do, and I love that I'm able to support myself and my family doing independent work. But, it took me a while to get here, and it hasn't always been easy. I've made sure that I'm proactive about my career and what I want to do. I kept an eye out for roadblocks and I was motivated to blow through them when necessary if I encountered them (which I have). Never content to be stuck without any options; early in life I learned to push to be heard and I re-evaluated my circumstances often so that I made a habit of making decisions, even the tough ones, when it became necessary. I constantly asked myself if this is who I want to be and what I want to do.

I mentor a number of people, and for most of them, the issue is finding out who they are and the values that drive them. Once they learn to grow through that, they can start to ask themselves what they want to do. They can build a career that mirrors who they are and what they believe in. It's not an easy process; it takes a lot of time and some serious thought. But it helps you get locked in to what you want to do with your life and enables you to start taking the steps to match your values to your work. There aren't many people who confidently map the two, most just go along for the ride and build a narrative that suits them, but there's still that gap. There's a missing piece they keep trying to identify but can't quite pin it down. Something just never feels right, and find themselves in limbo or never quite happy.

That doesn't have to be you, this isn't easy, but all that's holding you back from being who you want to be is you. And reinvention is an option... that's a leadership choice you can make for yourself.

The mulligan is yours; take it if you want it.

Getting Leaders to Own Their Role in Talent Management

In corporate America, leaders and executives often forget that their leadership objective is not only to manage the company processes, or to supervise the production of widgets. Their role is essentially made important by their charge to lead people. As executives tasked with running a company that is a fundamental and critical component of business that you cannot push off or delegate and expect that someone else has it covered.

Most executives consider talent management a Human Resources (HR) function and as such, best left to the leaders in HR because it's part of their duties to support the company in that effort. The truth is that for talent management to be pervasive and effective in an organization, the primary responsibility should be placed in the hands of the direct managers of employees. Most companies don't formally expect this of their managers and executives so it's not surprising they don't, and don't know how to do it. This is a void that not surprisingly becomes filled with mistakes and development of problems and issues that could have been prevented or certainly mitigated.

It's important for organizations to realize this and make a change in what tasks with respect to talent management are the responsibilities of management. Innovative companies that thrive and grow, have leaders at all levels that know they are responsible not just for managing their budget and numbers, but also for the people that work for them—understanding where each person is in their development, and how to best either keep them engaged in their current position, allow them to be seen as that key person in the role, productive for the good of the company, or prepare them so that they can flow to the next level.

When you get to be a senior director, or VP, in my opinion, your job should be focused on helping to build the bench strength of the organization. And that starts with your own team. If you are a leader, your primary job focus should be leading people. That cannot be seen as less important than balancing the department budget. You are on the front line managing the talent of the organization.

Let's apply the widely used 70-20-10 model to this discussion. If you are a leader, your work breakdown should match the development percentage mix. You should be spending 70% of your time developing your people by giving them challenging assignments, spending 20% of your time on coaching and mentoring them around both tasks and behaviors, and spending 10% of your time ensuring that they received the needed training to be effective in their jobs, or growing their knowledge through learning and development. In reality, in many organizations it's the other way around. I know this from my own experience.

At one organization, I spent seventy percent of my time doing administrative work, twenty percent coaching and mentoring people, and ten percent leading them—because I was told that by doing my administrative work I would be seen by those people as a good leader. That's not how it should or did work in my opinion. I was instead seen by my direct reports as the executive whipping boy, jerked around by my leader and forced to do tactical work outside of my area of expertise that I was hired for. (Something I expect others have encountered in their own careers climbing the corporate ladder.)

Regardless of what the job description read, or what I was told in multiple interviews, this was—in reality—not a leadership role. I was being mismanaged as a high potential, as top talent. I found myself seeing all the classic signs of being stuck between the job I was hired to do, and the role I was being allowed to play. Well, I did not stay stuck for long. A confluence of circumstances helped me make up my mind and served as the push I needed to make my way out of a valley of career despair.

Talent management needs to be seen as every leader's responsibility and they need to be equipped with how to manage that talent. They need to know (or be shown) what that effort looks like in the context of their organization remembering that each organization is unique. A set of metrics could be established so leaders understand that this is important to the organization.

* * *

The Conference Board recently put out its 2012 challenges for CEO's. Top two on the list: innovation and talent.

This makes complete sense to me. The world is changing rapidly as globalization keeps chugging along, and there's a huge demographic shift underway. We know this already; change is the only constant, and the ability to deal with it is the source of your "mojo" if you have been a successful leader for any time at all or feel you have what it takes to become one.

If you can't see what's going on externally, you can't react and respond... you can't plan or be proactive. If that's the case then how can you add any value internally?

Where is the innovation in human capital strategy? Most organizations are very good at HR tactics, but not so good in the critical discipline of managing and developing human capital (which is just as important a resource to an organization as is financial capital). And sadly, no amount of heroic HR tactics will make up for a lack of a proactive human capital strategy. We've been slow on the uptake in most cases. Most organizations are still developing their talent management systems, only a few have matured to a point where it's become fully integrated into the business. And almost all organizations consider talent management as simply the annual performance review process. So why isn't there something new to take its place? A few thought leaders in this space are doing a good job trying to shift the paradigm, but why aren't more of us really trying to push the envelope of becoming value added to the business?

There are technologies that exist for us to do some incredible things. The data is there for us to leverage, but in most cases it just sits there in a latent state, or worse, it's there in multiple systems that don't talk to one another. In a previous life, I was with a company that had a learning management system that didn't speak to either the performance management or the human resource information system or HRIS.

Why and how did this huge oversight continue to plague the organization? Why didn't someone in HR sound the alarm to strategically gain the advantages of using these smart systems to develop strategic people solutions? The reason is a simple two-word answer... leadership failure. Because HR leadership saw these as merely independent systems, and not as critical building blocks of an integrated talent management system. Once again "being strategic" was staring them right in the face, and they did not recognize it. A failure to recognize external influences and changes that will surely affect the business and organization coupled with not fully understanding or utilizing what is at hand to become a more effective and efficient company is the height of leadership mismanagement.

It's time for a change of direction, focus, identity and ways to contribute. Leaders should never have (or be creating) the reputation that they're the "act only when asked" type of leader. As professionals, we should look to innovate and provide ROI on our work to our business partners. To do that you have to be forward-looking and forward-thinking. Those are the determinants of taking proper action even if it means a new direction. If we can't do that as a leader, we will never add real value to our organization. Chase all the convoluted key performance indicators (KPIs) you want, they all come down to either making the organization money or saving the company money.

So go out and be bold, try new things, fail fast, fail cheap, and don't be afraid to take a mulligan (do it again until you get it right). And if your culture doesn't support (or reward) that, then you have decisions to make. Because that is a clear sign your culture is stuck in the middle enduring the shocks of failure to move beyond the same old tactics—the kind that can lead to atrophy or decline (two things that do your career no good).

In Today's Workforce... A High IQ Isn't Enough

In a recent study by Price Water House Coopers, 53% of CEO's said that they see a lack of skills as a major challenge facing their organization. So, what's being done about this? Has your organization made any significant changes to train your employees? Are you investing dollars in the learning and development functions? Or are you hoping that benign neglect will eventually work for you and that the university system will start pumping out more highly qualified employees than ever?

It's not just CEOs who are worried about the skills shortages. Employees themselves feel the pressure to upgrade their own capabilities. According to an Accenture report, The Learning Enterprise, nearly 55% of workers feel pressure to acquire new abilities. But here's the catch, only 25% of them actually feel like they are getting the support that they need from their organizations.

It's simply not working. We're not preparing for the future if we don't invest in the present. I recognize that this is a shared responsibility that needs to be tackled from the earliest levels of education all the way through corporate learning initiatives. The fact is we need to start acting differently if we're serious about taking on this challenge. Doing what we've always done isn't working. It's time for a new approach; one that balances public and private partnerships to develop a flexible and agile workforce.

There are ways to accomplish this. If we're serious about changing the way we operate, which will eliminate shortfalls in a skilled workforce, we need to value and reward the right talents and behaviors.

We know for certain that behaviors are what drive results. We also know they are driven by emotions. Emotions are contagious. Though we may not consciously give attention to it, within the social aspect of the work environment we have an open loop system that allows emotions to spread quickly. (Keep this in the mind the next time you see a group of kids giggling in a park, watch how quickly the laughter spreads. Or conversely, watch how quickly kids gang up on one another or form cliques.) When groups of people work together, they create a micro climate. This climate is impacted greatly by the emotions and behaviors of the 'leader.' Leaders have significant influence on our ability to perform and our capacity to adapt to new challenges and new stressors. The point is, IQ isn't enough anymore. We need to start embracing emotional intelligence and we need our leaders to do it now.

We also need to embrace learning agility. We need to start teaching our kids and our employees how to become intellectually curious. We need to adopt a new standard for how we view intelligence. And we need to reward individuals who are curious about not only the 'what' but the 'how' and the 'why.'

From a skill perspective we need engineers, scientists and mathematicians—right brain functions. This is nothing new, not earth-shattering news. We need human resource professionals that can develop talent and create cultures that support, recognize and reward the correct behaviors for those right brain thinkers but don't leave out the left brain thinkers. Most organizations rely on or would function much more effectively with a diverse group of people with different capabilities in a proper balance or proportion suitable for the organization.

We need teachers who open people up to learning and development resulting in well-trained highly detailed oriented personnel and those that are highly creative—again, in the mix that is appropriate for the purpose of the organization.

In a world where talent is growing scarcer by the day, we need everyone on board. We're selling ourselves short if all we keep focusing on is math and science. Yes, there's a gap there, but we're about to come into an age where there are skill gaps everywhere. The Boomers are leaving and will carry with them a lot of organizational knowledge and expertise. We can't afford as a society or as organizations to neglect that eventuality. We need to focus across the board. We need engineers who are politically adept. We need human resource professionals that are financially savvy. We need people to be agile. We can't afford to grow our workforce in silos anymore.

It's table stakes, get smart or get out.

We want people that can lead. People that have the emotional intelligence to flex when needed. People who understand how to forge forward in the face of uncertainty while continuing to motivate their people to follow. We need leaders who care and employees who are willing to try new things.

We can do this. A public and private partnership can help make this happen. We need to get into the schools early and work closely with the teachers, administrators and curriculum planners. We should be building curriculum that not only focuses on the hard sciences, but that also focuses on behavioral science. We should be teaching our people and our kids how to develop a curious mindset (perhaps to discover one that's there deep inside but neglected). One that questions and pursues knowledge. A mindset that isn't scared of the unknown and instead embraces it. One that sees the possibilities of the future. One that knows if we work together, on the right things, we can achieve greatness. A mindset that values intellect sees potential in the face of failure and one that embraces empathy as a key leadership trait.

Our CEOs have a right to be worried. But in that concern, should be an endless optimism that we can conquer this challenge and that we can rise together and embrace a new future and a new paradigm. We need true leaders to step forward and show the way.

Having A Personal Exit Strategy (leading the most important person of all)

This is about self-leadership. It all ties back into defining your core values, determining who you are and your self-worth both individually and as a member (employee, etc.) of an organization. Self-leadership really means self-determination. I'll put here two lines from *Invictus* (by the English poet William Ernest Henley) that you may be familiar with...

> *I am the master of my fate:*
> *I am the captain of my soul.*

You are those things only if you choose to be or set out to be. It's a choice.

There comes a period in your professional career when you are asked to give more of yourself than you may want. It's that point when you have to decide if you are a "company man" or if you are more rogue and independent. Are you willing to sacrifice to the long hours, commit to the endless politicking, and are you truly willing to give up a sense of self to "fit" within the company culture? There is no right or wrong answer here; each of us has a choice to make all our own.

Usually your gut will tell you early on if the company you are at is the right fit for you long term or not. You get a sense of the order of things, the expectations, the unwritten rules and you either decide to assimilate or you rebel. What you decide is up to you, but the results are not always within your control. If you choose to assimilate, it may be that the organization is not ready to acculturate you and take you into the fold. You may not fit the ideal corporate mold. Read the tea leaves early. I have talked a great deal about being stuck in the middle and the age-old question of, "Should I stay or should I go?" may be the most difficult place to find yourself in the company you work for.

Let's say you are ready to make the commitment, ready to sacrifice, prostrate yourself at the altar of the Company.... but what if the company is not as committed to you as you thought? You always need an exit strategy—a backup plan—even when things are going great. Even as the company continues to tell you you're high potential and have a lot of "headroom" or "runway" or whatever other buzzword de jour is used to imply, "stick with us you're going places."

I have watched it happen to too many good people. They are caught up in their own "hype" and they overvalue their stock in the eyes of the organization (remember what I said about conducting a true assessment—honesty starts with yourself). And then it hits, when something goes awry; a promotion does not come through or you are passed over for that great opportunity you were sure was coming your way. And you have not thought about what happens when what you expect doesn't turn out in your favor. What do you do then?

Do not get caught in this situation, always have options, always have an exit strategy. You never know when you may need it, and to not have one will leave you caught unaware—truly blindsided. If you are on the other side of this, the manager who's been espousing greatness and then pulls the carpet out from under someone who works for you—be aware of downstream impacts (remember the open loop system that exists within all companies). News travels fast.

Your true high potentials always have a personal exit strategy, understanding that and having one for yourself is a must in today's world to be an effective leader.

When Leaving What Do You Gain from Exit Interviews (Nothing)

Stop wasting your time chasing people for answers as they walk out of the door. If you want to learn more about your company, stop asking the ones who left about why they're leaving and start asking those who stay why they're still here (the Stay Interview).

Every exit interview that I've seen is subject to questions about validity. You can classify the attitude of employees who are leaving an organization into a few categories:

1. Disgruntled and angry
2. Bored
3. Ambitious
4. Extremely happy

Each of the above raises questions of soundness for me. If you're overly ambitious, why would you ruin any chance of coming back to this organization? If you're disgruntled what you say may be fueled by anger at one individual and needs to be examined carefully (not that it can't be right, but be careful using it solely). The point is it's tough to craft an engagement strategy around this data. You're better off conducting stay interviews. They are simple enough to conduct. To do them successfully you need to build a culture of trust and the interview should remain anonymous. They work best conducted once a quarter with a sampling of your employee population. In the interview, ask the following questions:

1. What is it about our company that keeps you here?
2. What type of offer would it take to lure you away?
3. What would cause you to leave?
4. What do we need to do to retain you?

The challenge here is that you need to get your employees and your leaders to understand what's said is used only to better the culture. With guarantees that it won't be used for retribution. Let's be real, if a competitor came knocking, most employees would at least listen. This is your opportunity to hedge and see what you'd have to do to keep your employees around and engaged. Once you get the data back, start looking for trends and make commitments to follow up and take action to build a better culture. If you're committed to running these once a quarter, you'll get a true sense of how your people view the organization and what you need to do about it.

Running at Warp Speed

Your leaders are running at warp speed—perhaps you are, too. Oftentimes too busy to get away for a lunch, too busy to make it home on time for dinner and too busy to coach that little league game.

There is a reason Google offers free dinners to its employees. They know they are pushing the envelope and testing their limits and their capabilities. The little things that they do for their employees have proven to be why Google is such a popular company to work for. Rewarding in different ways becomes the differentiator that makes them stand out and inspires those who work for the company.

So beyond free dinners, what could you do to inspire not only personnel but your leaders and managers?

What does inspired leadership look like in your organization? Are your people motivated enough to motivate others? Do they find the time to breathe, reflect, reset and re-energize? Do you even give them the opportunity to do so?

A candle burning at both ends burns out twice as fast.

If your key people are melting down (or in danger of doing so) invest time and resources to rejuvenate them and to instill the belief that their hard work pays off, not just for the company, but for them, too.

Take your leaders off-site. Get them away from the grind. Talk about business strategy. But also talk about them. Be attentive to their needs. Inspire them and give them time to reflect. Challenge them with new ideas and take them to new places. But have fun with it and let them breathe as you motivate them to return to work and become even more effective leaders. Help them find the purpose and the meaning in their work that will allow you to retain their talent.

Do not channel an inner Ebenezer Scrooge when it comes to planning this event. These are the people most responsible for your bottom line. Treat them right and they will treat the organization right.

Make a ripple with them and their people feel it as a wave. Remember though, a wave can lift you or it can sink you; just make sure it's the right vibe you want pulsating out to the other employees. Inspire your leaders. They deserve some attention too.

CHAPTER ONE

The Complexity of Culture

"You can easily judge the character of a man by how he treats those who can do nothing for him."

—Malcolm Forbes

Why Culture Matters More Than You Think

There is a growing body of work that discusses organizational culture as the catalyst for innovation and success. And it's more than just talk. In fact, the goad for the discussion comes from witnessing the successful examples set by companies like Apple, Starbucks, Nordstrom, Disney, L.L. Bean and Zappos. Look closely at them and you see culture matters. (Take Nordstrom and their unwavering commitment to customer service. It is so ingrained into their DNA that they will never deviate from keeping it front and center—they know that if their customers are happy they remain customers.)

Each of these companies has a very distinct culture. They target an area of their operation, make it their core strength and do not waver. Employees are hired, trained and measured on it and leadership reinforces it daily.

As we learn more about the importance of culture in an organization we realize it is no longer just a "soft" science. If it can be defined in a concrete form or fashion, why is it most companies cannot seem to get it right? They struggle mightily trying to create a vibrant philosophy that captures the essence of the company's personality and products or services. For many, their attempts have fallen flat. Millions of dollars spent on consultants and programs to discover or create their corporate culture and then to make actionable in a practical way within the company's operations so it permeates through all personnel— resulting in the same success as the companies they hope to emulate.

All good intentions, but why do the majority of these change initiatives fail?

From my perspective, it's because of three fundamental reasons:

1. Lack of buy-in and commitment from executives
2. Companies are too focused on short-term gains (true change takes time)
3. Employee fit

Let's focus on #3 for now. You can learn a lot about an organization by looking at their hiring practices and how aligned they are to the core strategy and the corporate culture. Most companies know how to spot and hire for talent. But that's only a piece of the overall puzzle. Fit is even more important. And few organizations really understand how to recruit for fit.

The demographics of both the talent pool and customer base are changing. Attracting the best talent requires new knowledge, skills and competencies. Hiring managers and recruiting staff need an awareness of where to find a diverse talent pool, how to effectively interact with candidates, and how to assess talent when it comes in a "different package."

Leaders now more than ever need to explore their own biases. Including an examination of the difference between personal preferences and job requirements and the impact of biases (both conscious and unconscious) and preferences on hiring decisions. They must examine what it takes to achieve "fit" in their organizational culture and how this information is communicated to candidates and new hires.

Managers tend to look at candidates in a vacuum.

They see talent and experience and think they are golden but don't take the time to probe and ask the questions that will truly tell them if this person is a good fit or not. As a result, they hire people that are good performers, but are not necessarily committed to the organizational culture. Eventually this lack becomes evident and it all rolls up to become an issue. The employee eventually moves on, or begins to underperform because they sense they don't belong, which possibly (probably) leads to a termination. Then we are right back at the beginning. A person to find... a position to fill.

Smart leaders recognize culture matters. Do it right the first time, and thank yourself later.

A Tale of Two Cultures

There are two cultures that exist in your organization today: formal and informal. Contrary to what you may think... it's the informal one you should be thinking about. Think of the formal as the body of a car... it's what everyone sees from the street. But it's the informal; the fuel, engine and transmission that make the car go.

It's in this informal culture space, within your company, where most people operate. It's where people talk (fuel) and where, importantly, people feel (engine). It's where work gets done (the transmission).

Your informal culture is more nuanced and more susceptible to change. If you're putting all of your effort into your formal culture and neglecting the informal, you're missing the boat. Even worse, if your formal culture is completely out of touch or misaligned with the way things really work, then you are shoveling BS to and on your people. And trust me, they know it.

We've all seen and experienced it: the senior leader(s) so heavily focused on the vision and mission they're not paying attention to how things really operate. Sometimes they're too hung up on titles, conventionalism and bureaucracy. This is when work breaks down (the transmission gives out), trust erodes (you run out of gas) and the negativity can become pervasive (the engine has fouled injectors). It becomes a vicious cycle that breeds further negativity that spreads to the informal culture. Once this happens, things can get away from you pretty quickly. Everything gets analyzed... every interaction, every subtlety and every decision. You end up paralyzed; unable to compete in the business race because "your car just won't go."

So be aware of your informal culture and be cognizant of what's around you and how you interact with everyone, because you're under a microscope. Don't forget the little people and don't play favorites with your folks. Don't let this undermine your team, your good work or your formal culture. Be aware, be alert and most importantly, be real. Because your informal culture is, and if you're not, it's going to be known.

I saw this play out with a friend recently. A senior leader of the organization happened to meet two people she knew and chose to focus her attention on one of them (giving a hug and a hearty hello,) while only briefly acknowledging the other (a glare and a hollow 'hi'). How does that play in the informal culture? What's the story that morning on your floor now? It's that you don't care about all your people, you play obvious favorites and worse you may be perceived as fake.

That Informal (Not Infernal) Network

This is important enough to business leaders (again, who often don't know of its existence or know and don't care—which is dangerous for their companies) to discuss further.

A recent article by John Kotter in the November '12 issue of Harvard Business Review discussed the duality of organizations; the formal and the informal network I touch on above. It made me think further on how, within each, there are nexuses of power dynamics that arise. In the traditional and more formal organizational structure, you have command and control. People gain power based on title and place. In the informal organizational structure, the network, people gain power through information and connections. What Kotter does, that was so thought provoking for me, is name this distinction, and he challenges companies to accept the distinction and to embrace it. He talks about creating a dual structure where the network is uninhibited by the formalities of a hierarchic command and control structures.

The challenge for most companies is that people are resistant to change, and 'creating' an informal network focusing on strategy that isn't controlled by a formal hierarchy is a ripe target for resistance. The irony is, it's already in place, you just haven't named it, and more importantly you haven't sanctioned it. It operates like a *favela* in Rio. You know it's there, it's impossible to miss, but because the law hasn't endorsed them, they operate under a veil of secrecy. But here's the catch, they're organized. They have structure and rules, they have guiding coalitions that are responsible for the upkeep and in that way they gain legitimacy. So the question is what's taking you so long? Why haven't you named it, approved it and used the informal network to inspire and engage your people?

Maybe you just haven't paid much attention to its existence.

Maybe you know it's there, but you refuse to believe in its inherent value or worse... you actively curse it. You do that because you don't 'get' what it really is... you have an outside view that misses the important point (that it's a valuable part of how your business really works).

Whatever the case, it's time you embraced it.

If you're unsure, of what it looks like ask people in your organization how they get work done. Do they go through the formal hierarchy, or do they work around people? My bet is they move around the established (formal) structure to get work done. Are you sending out notes to people telling them that they have to notify the formal leadership team before talking 'above' their station? If so, it's right there in front of you. You can't stop it, so name it, sanction it and use it!

Don't Get Worked Around

As mentioned previously, when people do not have confidence in the way their management wants things to work. Or when working through the people or within the framework of the system they are supposed to leads to nothing but frustration; they will find an informal way to get their work done. (And think about this. Isn't it those people who make the extra effort to get the job completed; despite the shortcomings of your company's formal system—who are the ones most important to your company?)

For those of you not perched in a corner office, with a "C" before your title; are there people in your organization that you'd rather not work with? And, I don't mean because you don't like them personally or you had some falling out with. What I'm talking about is they stonewall initiatives, they are roadblocks or refuse to offer any help when it comes down to getting things done. They'd rather pull out the job description and tell you that they're really sorry that wish they could help, but... it's just not their job. Do this enough times and I'm sure you will start to dislike them personally. But, if you care about YOUR job, what's most likely is that you will learn to work around them.

Working around people is a clear sign of a dysfunctional team. It's an indication that you have an informal network in play. Which, in and of itself, is not bad, but in this type of situation, it's clearly the result of negative behaviors. When it becomes commonplace for people on your team to say, "It's easier to do it myself than it is to work with that person," you clearly have some leading to do. (Hopefully it's not you that they are working around. Because if it is, then you have a team that's gone rogue and for your own well-being, you need to get a grip on things quickly and work out how your team can work with and not around you.)

If you start to see patterns where people would rather beg for forgiveness than ask for permission when working with you, take it as a clear sign, they're not buying in. They don't trust what you're asking them to do, or they don't see you—as part of the machine... the system—as a viable part of the process of doing the work and getting things done. This, friends, is office politics. It happens every day, in every company. The question that you need to ask is: "Am I in the way of getting work done?" Are you the reason that politics are being played and are you the reason that there are dysfunctional teams running around your building?

Culture Change 101: Hit Leaders in the Wallet

You may have noticed by now that I believe so strongly in leadership effectiveness that leaders should have their compensation tied to doing it well. Every initiative that has succeeded or been supported in the organizations where I have worked was because it was tied to compensation or bonus percentage payouts. Hitting leaders in their wallet is sometimes the only way to change a tough organizational culture for the better and making your organization (or the people that report to you) more effective is a direct result of a cultural improvement.

Leadership is not hiring the best and brightest and expecting that because they are so talented they will just figure out the right things to do. It is not allowing someone to fail at meeting expectations because the leader was too busy to share what those expectations are upfront.

Leadership is not letting an employee feel isolated because the rest of the team speaks a language that no one shares with the new employee.

Truly talented people have options and absent adequate leadership those options when exercised see those talented people depart your organization. Not for more money, but for greater appreciation of and use of their talent. They leave for greater "civility and respect" from another employer—someone who can lead them to the next level of accomplishment in their career. The cost it takes to make this realization and drive this truth through the organization is far less than the money flying out of the revolving door of hiring and losing people.

I'm not saying this model will preclude a company from ever having to hire talent from the outside, because the business is going to change over time and that might be required. But continuing to hire from the outside, while never taking time to assess their internal talent management resources, creates an environment where Gen Xers in the organization believe they don't have any future with the organization, and they start looking elsewhere.

And it's happening in most companies. When you ask CEOs "What are their organizations suffering from?" The issues of poor talent management and lack of leadership bench strength are among the most frequently mentioned issues. As organizations continue to get flatter and try to do more with less, they expect their HR professionals to handle all aspects of the culture change.

Implementing a cultural change, when done right, is a true strategic resource function owned by the lines of business, in the language of the business. For this very reason, in my opinion, it should not be considered solely an HR responsibility. It's truly analogous to supply chain management. Figuratively, if you had to look at an X-ray of an organization, what's the one part that would connect to everything and hold it all together? What connects the divisions, to the departments, to the mission, to the vision of the organization? It's the backbone. And in this analogy, that backbone is made up of the people of the organization. What do the people of the organization look to for the health and well-being of the company and expect—effective leadership.

Why aren't executives more focused on ensuring that there is an integrated, cohesive effort to attract, engage, and retain what connects every part of the business and thus sustains the organization's existence? Simply put, they are stuck in the middle between saying that "our people are our most important asset" and acting like it. And, because no one yet has come looking for their wallets.

Here's a scenario to give some thought to: At one organization, at the end of each year, they do a survey of the direct reports of each Director and above to find out how well they feel that they've been managed by their leader through the year to come up with a fair overall assessment. And that becomes twenty-five percent of the leader's bonus structure. That is taking becoming an effective leader seriously. That is the point when the leader would see talent management as their responsibility and to not push it off as, "That's not my job, that's HR's responsibility."

No—it is your responsibility. You need to change your effort from being a 70% doer of tasks, to being a leader for 70% and a mentor and a coach for another 20%. Using straight addition, 90% of your time should be developing the current bench for the future needs of the organization. That's leadership.

I feel so strongly about leadership and talent management that I believe leaders should have their compensation tied to doing it well. Every initiative that succeeded or was supported in the organizations where I have worked was because it was tied to compensation or bonus percentage payouts. Hitting people in the wallet is sometimes the only way to improve a challenged organizational culture for the better.

I'll repeat this because it's very important: Talent management is not hiring the best and brightest and expecting that because they are so talented that they will just figure it out. It's not allowing someone to fail at a meeting a leader's expectations because the leader was too busy to share what those expectations are upfront. Talent management is not letting an employee feel isolated because the rest of the team speaks a language that no one shares with the new employee. Truly capable people have options. And those options when exercised see those able people depart your organization. Not for more money, but for greater appreciation of their talent. They leave for greater "civility and respect" from another employer.

I've traveled to 36 countries (more to come) and visited several World Heritage Sites of special cultural or physical significance. The cost it takes to make this realization and drive this truth through the organization is far less than the money flying out of the revolving door of hiring and losing people. I'm not saying this model will preclude a company from ever having to hire talent from the outside, because the business is going to change over time and that might be required. But continuing to hire from the outside while never taking time to assess their internal talent management resources, creates an environment where Gen Xers in the organization believe they don't have any future with the organization, and they start looking elsewhere.

Continuing to reach outside for what you should develop within is a sign of weak leadership. And ironically, it's something that can be readily fixed and leadership strengthened, which has far reaching impact for the business and organization externally and not just within.

Eliminating Machiavelli

It's not 1532 (or 1970 for that matter) anymore, so stop leading like it is. *'Tis better to be feared than respected"* isn't a game you should be playing with your people. Machiavellian guidance doesn't cut it in the corporate world today, even if there are holdouts and apostles still trying to pay homage to it.

It's time to get into the 21st century and inspire your people.

If you're the type of leader who likes to create an environment of fear, I have news for you, you've lost. Gen X and Gen Y don't want to work with you. It doesn't matter how smart or successful you are (or think you are). If the environment you've created breeds fear, you won't get anything of substance from your people.

Let your people breath, take your foot off of their neck. If you don't think their smart enough to handle it, then why hire them? If you've inherited someone whom you think can't cut it, help them. If you can't do that, be real with them and let them know that it's time for a change.

If you're stuck on the little things, not seeing the big picture and not being empathic with your people you're going to lose them. Don't create a culture that kills creativity, or you'll lose your credibility with them. If you want to get your people to work with you, instead of for you, here are a few suggestions.

First, take note of *with* you, not *for* you. Your people don't want to work for you; they work for themselves, for their family. They want to work with you. So inspire them, lead them and get out of their way.

As a leader, you're responsible for the What, Why and When. Let your people manage the How (more on this later). Let them amaze you. You would be surprised at how quickly you build commitment, how easy it can be to inspire creativity and ultimately what kind of an impact this has on the culture that you build in your work group. Machiavellian leadership was great in an era of feuding princes and the fear of peasant uprisings, but we've come a long way since then.

Those that lead today by fear may just be acting out of fear themselves; the fear that their people will learn that they don't really know how to lead at all.

Action or Events

How do you manage your high potentials? Do you recognize them publicly? Do you put them into a development program? Or, do you make assumptions about what they know? If you do either, that's a good start, but it's not everything. You cannot end it there with the event. It's the next set of actions that you take that are most relevant.

I have a fairly regular conversation with a friend who was recently through a high potential development program. The program was 9 months long and they met three times during those months. In between they worked on two projects: one in the community and the other on internal process improvement.

He loved the program; thought it was great and came away re-engaged and ready to make a difference.

It took less than three months to undo. The event was awesome, the learning was great, but three months later when it came time for his annual reviews he got the "standard meets expectations" and a 3% raise. Now, I'm a firm believer that potential and performance aren't necessarily mutually exclusive, but they didn't message effectively at all. He came out of that program told he was the top 2-3% of his level. He had been in his role for well over a year and a half. His scope had not changed in that time either. So when he comes to the table, what was on his mind? What were the expectations that he should have? Entry into the program required high levels of both performance and potential. Didn't that merit a better review and raise? Where did it all go wrong for him?

Here's how:

1. Expectations weren't aligned with standard HR practices during the program
2. HR practices aren't aligned to the high potential development programs
3. Company-wide the focus was on the event and not the action
4. Manager was not having fully transparent conversations with him

It could be any combination of these four things. But even with the best intent in mind, if you are not thinking and being empathic at the individual level with your high potentials you're missing an opportunity. You had him fully engaged and now you have him disgruntled. Be aware, be vigilant and remember that the action is more important than the event.

* * *

"The foundation of a great company is the way it develops people—providing the right experiences, learning from other people, giving candid feedback and providing coaching, education and training. If you spend the same amount of time and energy developing people as you do on budgeting, strategic planning and financial monitoring, the payoff will come in sustainable competitive advantage."

—Larry Bossidy and Ram Charan, 2002

As Bossidy and Charan state, the foundation of a great company is how it develops people—that means taking concrete action at and for the individual level. It only makes sense to develop and grow the most enduring asset that an organization possesses. If people and their skills are allowed to atrophy and decline, then the organization will soon follow that same fate. This is why it is folly to cut developmental resources drastically in tough times because the skills and persistence needed to overcome adversity often result from developmental and deployment programs.

Strong developmental programs send the right message to the employees of the company. These programs contribute to morale, engagement and productivity. We also know that if employees do not have an opportunity to further develop their skills and experiences they will become a flight risk.

The new employee compact with organizations is based on the concept of "employability." If an organization commits to developing and enriching an employee's skills and experiences, then the employee will, in turn, commit to the organization. The best security any person has is to continue to strengthen his or her skill sets for their next career step—either with the current organization or another. If companies deliver on the development promise, there is less reason for an employee to leave or seek another opportunity.

Compared to the cost of losing talented people, employee development programs are a bargain. They are a very cost effective investment for the organization to make when compared to the cost of being stuck between the time and the money to find a replacement.

* * *

I'm not a Notre Dame football fan. I'm a Michigan football fan. But what I do like about Notre Dame is their football team's tradition (and think of 'tradition' in the same way as we've been discussing 'culture'). There is a sign hanging over the locker room exit that says, *"Play like a champion today."* The players see it when they head to practice every day... and for every home game. That sticks in my mind. It makes me realize if you're going to do this leadership thing, if you're going to be a leader in your own right and seek to motivate and influence others, unless you can really inspire excellence, you're not going to be able to lead. My definition of leadership is simple: it's about connecting with people. You have to be in the right mindset to do that. You have to be ready to lead. That goes back to that *"Play like a champion today"* sign in the Notre Dame locker room. Each time they step on their homefield they see that message. What message do you see when you get up or go to work each day?

* * *

Just as there are positive examples and experiences that drive home how you feel (or should feel about leadership responsibility)... there are always the flip side of that. I recall being led by one particular 'leader' who was one of those folks that didn't really tell what they wanted or what they expected.

They left it to me to figure it out, which ended up me having repeat episodes of failure because I would try based upon what I thought this individual wanted. Only to find out that's not what they wanted. I'd try again and "no joy".... nothing was working out. I got to the point where I asked, specifically, "Listen; what does a good result look like? What do you want or expect. What is it you need from me?" What was so upsetting about that individual was their reply, "If you don't know what that is, then maybe you shouldn't be at the level I hired you at." Hearing that is not a good thing (but instructive of how not to lead) and is a real slap in the face. You're trying to do your level best. You're trying to be all that you can be, to borrow a phrase from the Army. Yet you're being led by someone who leads (by intent or lack of skill) through a culture of confusion and fear and, quite frankly, it's not really a word, but asshole-ism. Just to be someone who would rather see you bump your head against a wall over and over and almost laugh at your failings, rather than help you.

There are people like that in life, career and business and they will be obstacles preventing you from growing into who you could be. It left some scars on me and at first and caused some self-doubt. What's funny is that quickly subsided the minute I got away from that 'leader' and started to get positive feedback from my new leader. Feedback and direction that was quite the contrast from what I'd just experienced. The fact is my former boss was just an absolutely horrible leader and a narcissist who needed to be the only person of note and of worth in their universe. Watch out for those people who are so against the grain from all that leadership is supposed to be. Avoid them like the plague and if you are unfortunate enough to work for someone like that; do everything you can within your power to find another opportunity and somewhere you will have room to grow and someone to work for that will help you do it.

KEYS TO UNLOCK THE DOOR TO EFFECTIVE LEADERSHIP

1) Emulate a Winning Culture --- Model your success after companies like Apple, Starbucks, Nordstrom, Disney, L.L. Bean and Zappos. Find your core strength and make that the guiding principle of your culture.

2) Coach and Mentor to Cultural Fit, Not to Job Function --- Developing and sustaining a positive and productive culture require that people "fit". It's not just about talent or experience alone; you must make sure that the person you hire can align with the culture.

3) Make Being Informal, Normal --- Never disregard the importance of the "informal" aspects of your company. If you focus only on the formal, you are not paying attention to the thing that may be the most important driver of culture in your organization.

4) Lead from the Front --- Always be accountable for what you do as a leader. Often leadership failures hit those that work for you and for your company much harder than the leader(s). Leaders need to share the pain... so approach decisions feeling you have "skin in the game." This is one of the cornerstones of establishing and sustaining an authentic culture.

CHAPTER TWO

Who You Are / What You Should Be
King, Poacher (or Robin Hood)

"A leader leads by example, whether he intends to or not."

—Author Unknown

Who You Show As Yourself Starts on Day One

Fresh faces, with new ideas and aspirations have been hard at work for a couple of months. Some may be new employees, temps or permanents and some may be interns that are watching and hoping to be a potential new hire for your company in a tough economy.

So how have you wowed them? What has your "on boarding" plan looked like for these folks? Did you have one? Or did you just think it was good enough to give them a job in the first place and leave it at that? Let me say that I hope the sentiment is not the latter; leading effectively often means doing the right thing for all and not just some of the people. We all talk a good game about the customer experience, but the employee experience needs to be solid if you want to get the customer piece right. And it starts on Day One; even if they are "only" temps or interns. Here's a quick quiz, see if you can answer yes to each of these for company's Day One experience:

1. His/her name was at security so he/she could get in the building
2. You had an orientation session (a welcome meeting counts)
3. There was a mentor lined up to help them
4. Your new hire/temp had a desk and a chair or place to work immediately available for them
5. Your new hire/temp had a computer (it has to work to count) or the right 'tools' of their trade ready for their use
6. You had "real" work for him/her to start on

If you answered "Yes" to most (hopefully all) of the questions then you started their Day One showing a modicum of awareness and care (for their experience). They'll learn more about the company and its leaders in the days to come.

They will begin to see who you are and look for deviation from what you should be.

Checking the Box

As you think about the directives you're going to give to your business for performance planning, are you asking them to go through the process so that they can check the box? I've seen it way too often, companies ask employees to go through the performance process and all that we measure is a check of the box. You MUST confirm that you actually had the conversation. But does anyone care about the content of the conversation?

We spend a lot of time putting performance processes into place. We ask the business to spend a good deal of their time abiding by the process but when it comes down to it, are we really measuring the results of the process. Sure you have your percent of completion and your fancy 20-70-10 bell curve to show the distribution of performance ratings but what does that mean? What do you actually do with the data, how does it inform your HR practices, how does it impact the business? Do you use it solely for doling out compensation? Or have you thought about how you can use it for truly raising performance levels, and driving home the business.

There are a lot of great companies out there, and a lot of great HR shops, but we don't do enough to share best practices and we definitely don't do enough to innovate. It feels like we've been so concerned about getting a seat at the table, that we've done whatever we could to not rock the boat. I don't know if it's a complex that we have because we don't generate profit, but it's time to change that reality. We have a big part in adding value to an organization; we just don't always have the words or the framework in place to describe it. But maybe we should start calculating the dollars that we save the organization as a tangible benefit or perhaps we start looking at the impact that our new superstar hire has on the organization and we figure out how to show that value back to the organization.

Point is it's no longer enough to just check the box on anything that we do. It's time that we started to look at HR as a driver of the business, that we buy into the idea that people are the differentiators in any business. And remember people are our business.

Kingmaker or Poacher?

Are you a kingmaker, or a poacher who hoards your talent? Typically, the answer to this question is dependent on the organizational climate and whether or not cross-functional movement is supported by the organization. However, you can be the change agent. If you are wondering if you are a kingmaker, here's a quick guide to help decide for yourself:

1. You actively seek development opportunities for your people
2. You market your best people to other leaders
3. You encourage your people to look at other opportunities
4. You put your people in front of other senior leaders
5. You create the climate and then you get out of the way

If you answered "No" to most of the above... then you are probably not a kingmaker or surely the type of manager who worries more about protecting their interests or territory than about doing what's right for your people and the company.

But not all leaders are kingmakers. Some are what I like to call the poacher-hoarder. The poacher is the executive who consistently takes talent from others (which isn't necessarily a bad thing) but they don't return the favor of putting talent back into the supply chain. Instead, they hoard them; thinking that they can't survive without them, or that they would weaken their own internal support if they moved.

Typically, this behavior is found in organizations where movement is limited and executives have a tenuous grip on their position. It's usually a sign of insecurity and fear (two things that make it impossible for you to lead if that's where you stand or what people perceive of you).

Don't let your organization or your people get stuck with poacher-hoarders. This can wreak havoc on an organization's culture and is especially true for your high potentials. If they see limited mobility and limited opportunity, they're going to stop waiting and hoping for career success... they will seek and find it elsewhere.

I once had an executive tell me that the biggest compliment she received from her peers was when they wanted to take her people. These were her 'A' players and she was open to them moving every time. She knew she had a ready bench and knew that she would develop them just as she developed this group. This was done in an organization that had some processes in place for supporting cross-functional talent moves, but they weren't the norm. This executive was a kingmaker. Her people rose through the ranks of the organization. She beamed during our conversation about one of her 'star pupils' who ultimately went on to become the CIO. He was one of many who rose through the ranks and her pride was evident. People in the organization wanted to work with her because they knew she would push them, challenge them and develop them.

Or Are You Robin Hood?

This may be the most important job you have. You need to find a way to maximize the purpose of the work that your employees do. Especially Gen Yers, they tend to be more motivated by making an impact and having a broader purpose in the work that they do. You need to be able to draw out the connections in their day-to-day. Robin Hood was very good at connecting and had his Band of Merry Men. They did good things and were productive—maximizing their purpose (to steal from the rich to give to the poor) and fought against poor leadership (Prince John and the Sheriff of Nottingham). That inspires the people around you and makes them stronger.

* * *

As Daniel Pink talks about in *Drive,* you need to be a purpose maximizer and help connect their interests outside of work to the work that they do. It's not an easy task; it requires you taking the time with them to understand what drives them, what motivates them and where they find meaning and purpose not only in their work, but in the world at large (again, Robin Hood was adept at this). If you can draw that connection and make it clear for them, you'll be rewarded for the time you spend up front.

When Connecting With Your People:

Don't be afraid to give feedback. There's the perception that Gen Y is 'soft' and spoon fed. That they don't take well to criticism. It's just that, a perception. Don't be afraid to give them tough feedback. They need it. It gives them the opportunity to learn. And learning is what it's all about for this generation. They've grown up in the technological age, they may have the attention of a squirrel, but they also have an insatiable curiosity to learn. It's the result of growing up in an age when information about anything is only a click away.

Learn from them. They're smart, they're motivated and you can learn from them. Be open to their ideas. Give them the space to voice their thoughts. Teach them how to manage up, show them what a filter looks like and then let them roar, you'll be pleasantly surprised by what you get back.

When the turn comes... roles will begin to open and movement will return to pre-2008 rates. If you're a Gen X employee on the cusp of assuming a broader and more complex leadership role, you need to prepare yourself for how to lead. That requires that you understand how to motivate those in line to follow you.

Build organizational strength. What does your company do to build organizational strength and resiliency? Are there specific cultural and structural processes in place that enable your organization to stay fit and lean? If your organization were in a race would it be a marathon or a sprint? Would you consider your organization healthy? How would you measure the health of your organization? Is it how your employees feel about the numbers that you put up quarterly, customer feedback or any combination of the above?

It is our responsibility as leaders to help the business grow strong and healthy. We are responsible for ensuring that we have the right people in the right roles at the right time to make that happen. It's also up to us to determine the processes used to build and sustain collective knowledge of the organization. We need to partner with the business to determine if we should be sprinting or sustaining ourselves and our people for the long haul.

Organizational strength is useless if we cannot sustain our efforts over periods of time. Short and quick bursts of energy are useful when we want to get over the line, but in the long term it will just burn our people out. We need to find ways to support our people and to help them develop the endurance to power through when times get tough. There is a lot of great work out there where HR is leading the charge and building the support systems for employees. Organizational health is vital to organizational strength.

You cannot be strong as an organization without being healthy. This requires that you have the right people practices in place. Practices that empower your people; that make your leaders accessible and ensure your goals and incentives are properly aligned and you are developing your talent. If you can focus on the right variables you can build a healthier organization that can respond to the needs of your people, your customers and your stakeholders.

The Agile Win the Game (And Avoid Becoming the Game)

I was talking to a colleague of mine and we talked about a lot of different things—a very refreshing conversation. We talked my books, we talked about the Olympics, and we talked about the Mars rover and the incredible job done by the NASA engineers. Lastly, we talked about our work and career. The two of us (an entrepreneur and a corporate guy) talked about the erosion of company loyalty and how the job market seems to be picking up a bit. We also allowed ourselves to dream a little too... about the best moments of our careers.

He reflected on work experiences of his dad and the two-way loyalty that came with a job during his time. His dad worked at the same bank for over 40 years. Insane by today's standards, but yet there was something to be said about his dad's loyalty as an employee and in turn, the loyalty of company to his dad. His dad dealt with politics and BS just like anyone else, but there was an unwritten understanding that they would see things through and take care of one another.

What may be striking to most is that this colleague is a member of Gen Y, also known as a Millennial. You know, the generation that is labeled as not loyal, the generation that cannot sit still... or so we think. I was personally surprised when he told me a lot of his peers would love to go back to that era of stability.

He longed for the glory days we all have heard about and for some reading this—have possibly seen and experienced. The days when senior executives would bring kegs to the parking lot on Fridays. The days when food was served at every meeting... and the days when work stayed at work, never 24/7 or all-consuming, always connected and "on."

Then I realized that those good old days never existed for this generation. They started to enter the workforce when the Internet bubble was crashing and then 9/11 happened and the world flipped. Shortly after that it was the Great Recession, and now it is the never-ending recovery. Unemployment for this generation is higher than for any other generation right now. If you Google Gen Y unemployment, the top story lines are about their new reality: unemployment, living with their parents and an unsecure retirement. The prospects look bleak, but I have faith in our ability as Gen X leaders to build a better place for them to inherit. It cannot just be a game anymore, there is too much on the line. We need to help figure it out. Gen X cannot be on the sidelines anymore; it's our turn to lead. It's our time!

When the Game Slows Down

You know the feeling you get when you are really good at something and are in the zone? Everything slows and your focus sharpens. You feel invincible and it's a great feeling. But, it's not happening as often in the business world anymore. We are so inundated with change, innovation, progress, tasks—noise and static—and people that it's harder to find the leaders who are capable of getting into the zone. It's obvious by now that the game has changed for us. It's no longer what it was 25 years ago or even five years ago for that matter. So how do we adjust?

It takes some time and it takes some prep work. An analogy that I like to use is the NFL. The speed of the game keeps increasing, new rules and regulations have changed the style of the game and the way it's played, but we are seeing a movement of young quarterbacks who are coming in and immediately making an impact. It's pretty amazing to watch. Sure, they still make mistakes but they are learning on the job, and doing it quickly, and nothing is more important than game day experience. It's what enables them to grow and get better in the league. They get enough time under their belt and the game starts to slow down for them. Literally. They learn to process and filter all of what is going on around them more quickly and you see their game rise to another level.

As we think about our own profession and how we develop talent, what can we learn from the NFL? How can we build enough relevant playing time along the way for our up and coming talent so that by the time they get into the big leagues the game has slowed down for them? We want them to be making clear decisions and in this environment they better do it quickly. They cannot delay and need to learn how to process, interpret and react. And they better do it fast.

If we can teach them to get into the zone and help them learn how to exercise their brain, we will inevitably slow the game down for them. And that gives us all a better shot at victory.

Learning Agility

I get asked quite often about the one trait that I look for when assessing talent. Over the years I have dissected, analyzed, poked and scratched at the question. I quipped that it was dependent on the context of the organization, the role you were looking to hire for, etc. I thought I was being smooth and tactful. But in reality, I was being too political and not taking a stance. The reality, which I learned through all my years in talent management and leader development, is this: learning agility is the most important quality when assessing talent.

It is really clear in this new environment (post-2008), where weaknesses in the economy are still evident and the pace of change is at warp speed, that we need employees who are capable of learning on the fly, and have an interest in learning new and differentiated skill sets. It's imperative that we start building an ambidextrous (in the capability sense) workforce. Employees need to be ready to cope with change, learn new skills and deal with ambiguity if they want to succeed.

Employees, particularly Gen Xers, need to demonstrate learning agility if they want to thrive in our current workforce. It's no longer enough to rely solely on one set of skills. It's now a requirement to be diversified in your skills and to show a penchant to learn more.

This places a heavy burden on leaders and senior management. The executives of any organization are responsible for building the structures to recruit, identify and develop this ability within. It requires that we build a flexible model that supports cross-functional opportunities where people can share best practices and learn on the job. It also requires that we develop innovative ways for people to learn, that we refocus our efforts on learning and development, and that we challenge the practitioners to design spaces for people to learn in ways that we have not done.

We need to challenge the status quo and try new things. It's up to us to help cultivate learning agility as the prime factor for success in our work place.

The Essential Value Perception That Defines You

Will Your People Stay or Go

When the economy turns and jobs start to open back up, why will your people stay? What's going to entice them to stick around? If you've been forced to make cuts over the last few years have you checked in with your employees to see if they are still engaged, or better yet somehow inspired? The market is starting to loosen, your stars always had the option to jump; they just had to weigh out if the grass was really greener or not. You see, they have options; they have a network and most have feelers out.

Check your engagement strategy, because you're going to need one. And if you don't even have one, you should be working hard to create one, because that war on talent is not going away—especially in the face of a sustained recovery. If your engagement strategy is to just throw more money at your people (if that's even possible) you better think again. Daniel Pink talks a good deal about mastery, autonomy and purpose and in the knowledge economy where wages are competitive with the market rate; he shows us that monetary incentives actually decrease performance levels.

It's time to get more creative with your engagement strategy. If you haven't already checked out the big players in the space; the companies I mentioned elsewhere (Google, Zappos, Nordstrom, Starbucks), keep their employees happy. They empower them and create the space to allow them to get creative and try new things without risk of failure. Innovation is the corporate mantra du jour; innovate or die. So why is it our people innovations are so limited?

We have access to data, we know the essential components of leadership and we keep hearing that people are our key asset, so why is it that our people strategies aren't more cutting edge. How can we continue to engage our people with policies and practices that were created to support a different type of worker in a different era? It's time to think differently about how we engage and manage our people. If we don't we're in danger of losing our most valuable asset.

Changing Our Inheritance

At some point, Boomers will actually start walking out the door. Gen X will be asked to step up and lead. Once that happens, you need to fundamentally ask yourself about change. What kind of change will enable the organization to grow? What type of change is needed to engage your people and how can you create sustainable change that doesn't revert to the old? It's really a question of how do you make change in an organization that you've inherited?

Creating change at the organizational level of system is already difficult. Compound that with a leadership transition and it becomes even more challenging. It requires a great deal of tact. And it requires a strong leader to help get out in front of the change, to create the environment to support and foster the change and to build the space for people to effectively move through the various emotional stages of change.

People in your organization may tell you that change is needed and most likely they recognize that it's coming, but that doesn't mean they're really ready for it. You can't change people. They are out of your control. People need to change on their own, at their own pace and in their own time. However, it's possible and necessary, for you to change the conditions, the rewards, the processes and the structures in support of your change.

The reason most change initiatives fail is that the majority of plans take all of the physical and tangible elements into account, but they leave out the human element. The emotional and cultural components. The trap many of us fall into is that we don't buy into the idea that emotions and culture matter at work. We don't fully understand that simply changing the mechanics of an organization does very little to change the way people actually cooperate and interact to get work done. In times of stress we revert to our "in" groups. We become more of who we are, and we tend to search for familiar patterns.

As a potential leader of your organization, you need to recognize that change won't be easy. And most importantly, when it's time for you to make that change happen, you need to understand and recognize how people will interpret the change and how they will respond to it. You know you're intelligent, you know it's baseline for your role. And now with this raised awareness, you're emotionally intelligent enough to make this change work.

A Dip in the Talent Pool

Succession planning is all about reducing risk, and CEOs and Boards of Directors hate risk. Most organizations do not have an adequate pipeline of leadership talent and senior managers to ensure consistent operation. For these organizations, succession planning is the most significant business driver for talent management in organizations.

McDonald's (circa 2006) had two CEOs die or resign for health reasons within six months of each other. Successors were named right away but sometimes haste does indeed make waste—unless you've prepared your organization and your leaders for the speed of the decision. Poor succession planning has been linked to companies with revenue shortfalls and substandard performance. With senior leaders getting older, this is a continuing issue. Replacement planning fills immediate gaps but it is, at best, a stop-gap measure designed to fill a position quickly. Replacement planning is reactive, tactical and often of limited value. In some cases, replacement planning is the best option; but in most cases it's not.

Succession management looks beyond the immediate situation to a future horizon and therefore is more forward-looking and strategic. Development is also a vital part of succession management as leaders and managers prepare for the future. If management just wants to clone itself, then replacement planning accomplishes this goal. If management wants to adjust to the future, continuously improve and lead the organization in new ways (if it's determined that a new direction is what is needed), then succession management is the best process to follow.

Talent pools are increasingly the choice for succession management. A talent pool is when more than one candidate is being groomed for higher level positions. The talent pool provides greater choice and flexibility for the organization. It's increasingly difficult for an organization to groom a single candidate for a single position.

Remember the McDonald's example. A quick, ill-conceived and planned for choice sets the wrong expectation. The decision has to be made as the end product of the succession process after different candidates have been vetted. The talent pool construct also argues for more cross-functional skills and experiences. A candidate needs to do whatever he or she can do to be highly qualified for different types of positions. And companies must know if they are in the shallow or deep end of the talent pool before they dive in.

Minding the Talent Gap

It is time to take a critical look at your talent and start asking the tough questions. Is the talent that you have today ready to meet your business needs of tomorrow? It's not an easy question and it's fairly subjective, but you have to do it. Most importantly, you have to do it with partnership from the business.

A full-scale talent assessment requires that you spend some time conducting a SWOT (strengths, weaknesses, opportunities and threats) analysis in conjunction with the business. This creates alignment with your business and its strategic direction.

From this analysis, you should learn the overall direction of your company, its market and your competitive set. You will also be able to build out a plan for what the critical skill sets are that will help your company stay competitive in that space. Once you have this in hand, it's time to start looking at the talent and the skills that are internal to your organization. If there is misalignment you will have some heavy, but vital, work in front of you.

A surface scan of your talent can give you a general idea of what your perceived internal knowledge, skills, and abilities gaps are. But the challenge that most organizations face, when it comes to talent management, is that the systems and the data they have on employees are incorrect, or incomplete. We may know what roles they have held since working with us, and from that we can make assumptions about their skill sets, but that picture is not always comprehensive. Most organizations I have worked with did not have a clear view into what their employees have done prior to coming into the current organization.

This leaves a big gap, and potentially leaves us squeezed between whether to hire from outside, which may be costly or instead, looking for skills within the organization when visibility on that may be problematic. To prevent this from happening, consider building an internal skills database that allows you to see more clearly into what other skills your employees possess. It's our responsibility as leaders to do this for our people. We owe it to our employees and to the organization. You never know what you may find, and may be pleasantly surprised.

Do You Just Talk Or Actually Walk?

Walking the Development Talk

It is time to take leadership development to the next level. Time to really rally your troops. It is time that we recognize the value of developing our people. And it's time we stop taking the importance of development for granted. We need to stop allowing ourselves as leaders to sidestep our own development. We claim they are too busy... but I am not buying it. All of the research points to the good that comes when a leader jumps in front and leads the way. As leaders we are most admired when we take initiative and show their people that they buy into the idea of development as beneficial for them, and for the company.

While to many of us this is common sense, it's not common practice.

All too often, we talk about critical skill gaps. We talk about the need to develop our internal talent. But our leaders are NOT walking the walk. They are skipping right on by. Thinking that development is not for them, that they do not need the development. They act as if they have learned all they can learn, and with what little time they do have, it's eaten up by other responsibilities. I think this is shortsighted. Leadership development has now more than ever become critically important. Our top leaders even claim as much when they talk about the urgency of building bench strength and the competition for talent.

So leaders, listen up.

It is not enough to talk about developing your people. They need to see that you take it just as seriously. That development is a part of your own personal plan; that you are committed to learning something new, and that you are willing to remain open to the experience of learning. If you want your people to become up skilled, find the time first for yourself. Make time to learn something new and bring your learning back to your people. Take the lead by empowering and encouraging them to do the same.

For those of us in the leadership space, it's high time to start developing relevant and worthwhile learning initiatives. You need to find ways to better equip your current and future leaders, you need to shake up the way you do things and how you operate. It's time to start a learning revolution. Gain the buy in from the top and then drive it all the way down. Your most valuable asset is your people, which include you, too, as their leader.

So are you a leader who actually walks the development talk?

If not, what is keeping you from taking the first step in the right direction?

Building Your Team of Superstars

Great leadership requires more than a great vision. It requires self-awareness, humility, and emotional intelligence. Great leaders surround themselves with great people. They know they can't do it alone; they're self-aware of what works for them, where they have weaknesses and they create a climate around them that fosters success. Before you can even consider building a team of superstars, you need to reflect on yourself and the impact you have on those around you.

If you want to take your performance and your team's performance to the next level, create a climate that inspires others. Be aware, look around and engage your people, say hello... and wait for a response. If you build the foundation for your team's success, you'll see returns come more quickly. People want to follow, it's our natural instinct, we look to authority to help guide us, but we're fickle and highly opinionated.

As you begin to shape the climate of your team, look for opportunities to build a high performing team. The job market is starting to shake out and open up, people are starting to move around a bit, and building a strong team requires you have a good mix of diverse ideas, opinions and people. If you want A-players on your team, but currently feel like you have the B-team, it's time you start making changes to the roster.

Here's some ways to do it:

1. Look for other internal opportunities for people on your team
2. Craft development opportunities through work projects for your people
3. Work with other leaders to put together cross-functional teams
4. Learn who your internal talent is
5. Keep scanning the horizon to bring in new talent
6. Take a risk on someone internal that you believe in

Brian Uzzi of Northwestern and Jarrett Spiro of Stanford researched the success of Broadway shows by looking at the composition of the team that was assembled to create and run the show. Their findings have implications for how we assemble our teams and for talent management in general. Through their research, they were able to show success was dependent upon a mix of new and old blood and the group's ability to involve their former networks to get work done.

If you want to build a team of superstars, start first with yourself, become self-aware and set the foundation for success by influencing your climate. Then, start looking for a good mix of old and new, build a team that is resourceful, creative and networked. You'll see the returns if you play your part right.

What Is Your Essential Value Set?

As a leader, when's the last time you took inventory of your essential value set? These are the values that you hold most dear, the ones in which you'd never compromise, no matter the situation. Are you still holding true to them, or have they changed, and if they changed, why? What made you think differently, did you sell out, or did you have good reason to change? Think about this as a 'this I believe' exercise in leadership. It's how you want to conduct yourself, how you'll treat others and ultimately it's how others are going to view you.

Before you jump to what they are, take some time to think about the life experiences and people that helped shape those values. We all have someone or something that helped shaped who we are for better or worse. It's through these experiences and relationships that we draw our values. It's watching what's right and what's wrong unfold in front of you and coming to terms with how you feel about something and taking a stand. It's understanding how your vantage point of any situation influences your interpretation of what you see. There are numerous people and events in my life that have shaped me as a man, as a father, husband, and leader. I use these experiences to tell my story and I find common threads across my experiences that I use to relate to others.

I challenge you to do the same. Be real with your people, open up once in a while and let them know that you're human. That you have experiences you persevered through and give them that hook to latch onto. It's amazing to see true leaders interact with their people; they find ways to relate, they adjust their tone and message to accommodate level and experience, and they find beauty in the diversity of experiences and beliefs that others bring with them.

Most importantly, these leaders wear their values on their sleeves. It's not a question of what they will do or how they're going to do it, you already know, because they've been clear about what they believe in. And they hold true to an essential value set that works for them that is drawn from their experiences. It's what makes them real, and keeps them from being stuck in the middle of the pack. So learn from them, and then use those lessons to shape your own values.

* * *

I've worked hard in my career to learn how to be a good leader and have enjoyed the experience of people saying they'd love to work for or with me, or they'd love to be a part of my team. That used to make me wonder, do these people want to work with me because they think they'll have an easy time? Do they want to work for me because they're trying to get away from doing something they're supposed to do? Being much more experienced now I no longer ask that. I've found that most of those times, those people wanted to work with me because the people who I did have as part of my team, those I was leading, were talking about how well the team was run, how validated they felt, how empowered they were to actually accomplish things. It's interesting when you have people say, "I'd love to work with you even if it's on another project, or even if that means I have to add work to my plate." I think that's very telling from a standpoint that people really want to be led. They want to have someone who cares for them, sees them as a person first, and a way to get work done and achieve objectives and key performance indicators secondarily.

I always thought, first and foremost, about what it means to be led as well as what it means to be a leader. So that's what I would say to you—the reader—when you have people wanting to be led by you or wanting to be part of your team, don't think, as I originally did, that it's because they're looking to get out of something. Instead, take the time to seek out why that is. You might be pleasantly surprised to find that you're doing such a different, effective job at leading that others want to be part of what you're doing.

* * *

There were plenty of folks that I came across in my time in uniform that were good, salt-of-the-earth people, excited to be in the military, and who took their rank and their opportunity to lead very seriously. They did it from a perspective of trying to make everyone better, including themselves. But then there are some who were weasels that the minute they put on rank, wanted to push people around who were beneath that rank. Almost like the kid that got beat up every day on the way home from school becoming the town Sheriff or State Trooper and then goes around seeking vengeance on all who picked on him or dared to poke fun at them when they were growing up.

One guy in particular I met when I was in the Navy and had the opportunity to serve with onboard a ship. He and I were the same rank, but he was hell-bent on going officer. His whole motivation for becoming an officer was he hoped to, one day, be the leader of a division on a ship. Then he could, quite frankly, show those who had Chief Petty Officer rank how much of a jerk he could be to them because of how much of a jerk some of them were to him. I've seen that same type of personality in the private section—in my career and in business. I think that's the wrong way to go.

Revenge shouldn't be your motivation for anything. At best I think it's harmful and sad to hear and see that people have no other desire than to get back at others, and that's what they use to fuel ambitions. Do not be one of those people. If you have a desire, within some organization, to get some payback on others for some reason take the high road and do it through showing you are a superior leader because of the qualities of your integrity and character.

KEYS TO UNLOCK THE DOOR TO EFFECTIVE LEADERSHIP

5) Show Up The Same Way Every Day --- Who you show yourself to be starts on Day One. Give all employees (even interns, temps and new hires) the type of experience you would appreciate if you were in their shoes. That goes a long way to establishing how you are perceived as a leader and an organization.

6) Lead By Good Examples --- Be the right type of leader for your people and your organization. Kingmakers and poachers each have shortcomings that have a long-term negative impact on what you accomplish as a leader. Be a Robin Hood: form, inspire and develop your merry group of followers and workers—and your legend will grow (and so probably will your company).

7) Be Agile, Not Fragile --- You have to be flexible and willing to learn in order to be an effective leader. If you are intolerant—brittle with those you lead and can't see your way to make the right decisions because you're unwilling to learn and adapt—then your leadership will fracture. And you can't build a growing organization on a cracked foundation.

8) Be Genuine Always --- If you approach leadership genuinely without personal artifice and never convey an "I'm better than them" mentality then you can draw the best people to work for you. If you lead they will follow. How you lead them is what you leave behind as your legacy. It can either be something positive that propels them and your company onward… or negative that saps their strength and leaves organizational weakness.

CHAPTER THREE

The Impact of What's Missing

"Example is not the main thing in influencing others. It is the only thing."

—Albert Schweitzer

Leadership Vacuum (more Dyson than Hoover)

You are either of substance or you are not—which do you choose to be?

Depending on what you read and who you listen to, we remain in the middle of a leadership crisis. There are power vacuums across the political, social and business spectrums. Leaders apparently are in short supply. But is this really the truth of it? Are we witnessing a power vacuum or have we reached a point where the traditional notions of leadership don't align to the issues and challenges that we now face day in and day out. Our world has changed drastically, but in some ways, we're still tied to a framework that was built for the industrial age. It is akin to what we see in education, where instruction and underlying principles are still allied in many ways with the Industrial Revolution.

The leadership framework has to change; we are not playing in the same sandbox. Our challenges are different, the pace at which we move and with which decisions get made is incredibly faster than what previous leaders have had to deal with. Now, more than ever, we need savvy leaders and, yes, savvy followers with a better understanding of the issues we face and a realistic expectation. There is a very real disconnect, in many ways, between sound-bite hyperbole and what the actual issues are and who or what the obstacle to overcome is.

Power is now diffused across a greater spectrum than ever before. People have access to more information and more technology, giving them a voice that most people never dared dream of. Look at the Arab Spring, the Tea Party and the Occupy movements. There were no clear leaders per se, but each has left an indelible mark. The people rose as leaders and worked harmoniously to raise issues, overthrow dictators and bring awareness. The ends may still be in question, but we saw collaboration on a scale never before possible.

Power lies in networks and information in today's world. Leadership still matters, but our reality calls for a different framework for leadership; one that understands how leaders and followers interact in this new age. This framework needs to recognize and give credence to the fact that hierarchical structures aren't required for leaders to work or emerge in this global era. How they lead and what their leadership centers on and the results of their leadership and accountability for them are where the connected and informed followers need to render judgment.

Failure to Open (The Hearts and Minds of Those You Lead)

When Leaders Fail To Be Leaders

You can't have it both ways. You can't be all controlling, all knowing and all seeing until something goes wrong and then decide that you're not really accountable. It happens all the time. Especially at the top of the house (example: JPMorgan Chase's two billion dollar mess that their all-powerful leader never saw coming).

Jamie Dimon seems like a good leader, steadfast, bold, and courageous... with a touch of arrogance yet still comes across as likable. He's been known to go off the mark, he's also known to inspire others, and he led his company through the great financial meltdown. But, he's not infallible, and when it came time to take accountability for this mess, he passed the buck. You can't have it both ways. You can't be the omnipresent leader who gets into all of the details of your organization and then claim ignorance when a debacle like this occurs. The New York Times ran an article the day after the announcement, claiming that he was caught by surprise.

People that work in that organization will tell you that Jamie doesn't miss a beat when it comes to the details. His leadership team reports their financials weekly in the utmost detail. Two billion dollars is, by any scale of measure, a lot of money— attention getting money for even the wealthiest or most jaded of executives (companies or governments). Even if it only accounts for a tenth of their total worth that kind of money doesn't get lost on him. So how is it that when it comes time to take action it's his chief, Ina Drew that takes the hit? I'm not calling for his head;

Jamie's done too well with the organization. But, shouldn't he protect her? He stands up to others all the time, how can he let her get pushed out the door?

Aren't good leaders supposed to stick up for their people? Aren't they supposed to take the heat when things turn south? I don't buy the argument that he was surprised. He set the framework for the group in question to take ever larger bets. He committed to this strategy, for better or worse, but when it failed, he failed as a leader to be accountable.

There are lessons in good and bad leadership in this. Think about whether your actions as a leader are consistent and congruent with doing the right thing for your people and your organization. Failure to do so closes the door on reaching the hearts and minds of those you are supposed to be leading.

When Things Don't Go As Planned

You should always have a backup plan. Life throws curveballs, you will be caught off guard at times by the decisions that others make (and sometimes by the results of your own decisions). When things do not go as planned in your career, or with your company, the worst thing you can do is to be so surprised that you are out of options—a duck dead in the water—stymied. Do not feel trapped; do not get stuck in the middle (between where you want to be and where you're at).

How to Be Prepared

You should be building networks all along. Do not take anything for granted. I have seen it happen too many times to realize that you do not put all your eggs in one basket. Employees who are deemed high-potential and seem the logical choice for succession when the next level role opens up stop networking, discontinue having their career conversations and assume that role is theirs. Only then, something funny happens. The role changes, new leadership is brought in, or any numbers of variables change the assumed outcome and you are left out. You are told your time will come. So do you wait and hope or do you call on your network?

Truthfully, you do neither (though if you do have a network of contacts you'll surely scramble to tap them—but at that point you're at an 'after the fact' disadvantage. You should have been tapped into your network all along. You should always be having conversations about what opportunities interest you and what might be a good fit for you. This way you have leverage; you get to be picky (when the stuff hits the fan you won't have any and you may not have the luxury). You get to choose the option that is best suited for you and what interests you most. This is not to say you are constantly hunting for new work, you need to have patience, but you build a strong network for a reason. And you leverage it at the right time for the right reasons. You keep an eye on the horizon. You read the proverbial tea leaves and you cast your net far and wide. Most importantly, you NEVER turn down a job conversation.

When you start thinking about your career, you need to think about multiple paths, multiple options. Have an end goal in mind, but always be open to the journey and how you're going to get there. Life is full of possibilities; it's up to you to figure out which best suits you.

The Only Constant

"The only constant is change...that is the dominant factor in society today."

—Isaac Asimov

It feels to me like this holds especially true in the world of business, particularly in how we constantly look to institute new structures, new processes and new innovations in the hope it gives us an edge over our competitors. I've seen organizations introduce the newest and greatest management theory only to replace it a few months later with another idea. I've seen CEO's turnover frequently in organizations and each time one leaves another one comes in to implement their change agenda.

I'm not making a case that change is bad, but I am saying that for change to work, that is, for it to be sustainable, it needs to become a habit. And it feels like the only habit that we know right now is how to change. Not how to sustain it. We've been so inundated with the idea and the practice of change that we've become used to the idea that something won't stick. So automatically, we resist it. We undermine it from the start, because our brain recognizes the cues and we revert to traditional habits, which in this case is to shut down and switch into 'sleep' mode. It's a normal response. It's what allows us to drive home every night, or put on our clothes in the morning without going into intellectual overload. The irony is that we're so wired for change, that we don't let it play out because we expect it to fail or to get swept up in the tide of change and get pushed out before it even gets started, like so many of the initiatives before it.

Real change requires forming new habits; remember this the next time you want to roll out the management flavor of the week. Every time you roll out an initiative that doesn't stick, you undermine the chance of the next one actually working. It's like telling your people that you want leaders with performance and behaviors, but you go and promote the jerk that just manages to the numbers. It undermines everything.

Don't Go Over the Ledge

Mind the ledge over the deep dark pits. It's real and you can fall off if you are not careful. Pay attention. Do not get so caught up in the day-to-day drama that you trudge on mindlessly—inching closer and closer to the edge. Put the iPhone or iPad down for a minute. Pay attention. Open your eyes. Ignorance has consequences. Be mindful of the warning signs. They will not always be as apparent as a yellow sign, a metal rail, or a concrete barrier. But, the warning signs are there if you open your eyes long enough to look around for them.

In the workplace, there is not just one ledge to be wary of. There are a series. Organizational politics create pitfalls in unsuspecting places. Generational differences create chasms of misunderstanding for the unsuspecting to trip into. Interpersonal power dynamics create deadfalls that go unseen to the oblivious. Many even ignore warning signs at their own peril by moving forward too fast. My point is this... keep your head up and stay alert—danger awaits you.

The ledge has gotten each of us at one point in our career. We cannot avoid all of the many hazards. But as Gen Xers leaders we need to be alert to the set of expectations that comes with our age. And as we decided whether or not to live up to them, we sadly stepped wrong and got stuck, became apathetic—or worse we fell hard and far.

There is an expectation from Boomers that we as Gen Xers need to step up our game and lead in the manner that they have defined as leadership. There is an expectation from Millennials that we as Gen Xers will help them avoid the hazards, build them up, and help them succeed. But there should be an expectation for us; watches set for the risks that are surely in front of us, and forewarned, we can continue to find our own way to bridge over or go around them.

It is time for us as Gen Xers to push change, move organizations, and knowing where the perils lay, with a solution in hand help our colleagues past them. If we want to stay relevant as employees, we must be seen as contributing members of the organization. And ultimately, to take over as the leaders we are... we need to take calculated personal career risks and push forward. But as we do, we need to be mindful of the threats and all the mistakes waiting to be made so that we can avoid them and proceed undaunted.

None of us would choose to doom ourselves to free falling through an abyss of mediocrity for the next 20 years of our careers.

Mind the ledge Gen X... we have been warned.

* * *

One of the most important and impactful things I've done in my career is to always ask my team, at the very beginning of working with them or they for me, how they would best like to be led. I think the reason I ask that question is (1) I am not a mind reader, and (2) all of us need different things from our leader. I believe, also, that leadership has to be flexible. I'm a student of the concept of situational leadership as written and discussed by Percy and Blanchard and later by Blanchard only in Situational Leadership II. I believe there are different situations through which your leadership style can and should change. That should be dependent not only on the situation, of course, but also on the individual and what their specific needs are.

As I touched on above, since I long ago gave up trying to be a mind reader, I like to ask people. Once they get over the shock of having their leader ask them what it is they're looking for, how they'd like to be led, I've found is it allows everyone to get on the same page. The feedback that's valuable might be something like" "That's in line with a leadership style that works for me," or "It's not," or "It's something I can do," or "something I cannot do." By asking those questions up front, it gives you a leadership relationship of, quite frankly, credibility. It gives you a starting point to work from and room to grow. It minimizes the frustration and disappointment that comes when you try to use a direct leadership style on someone who prefers more of a hands-off leadership style.

Granted, I will say that folks have to try out different things and see what works best. And there are going to be times when somebody says, "I would prefer a very hands-off leadership style," but then you look at their work and how they do things, and you realize that, more than anything, they need a hands-on leadership style to get them to do what they need to do. When you have the opportunity, look and try to make the match between who that person is or what that person says they want or need in a leader, and who you can be. Because I think, it'll bring an ease and a flow and flexibility to your relationships as a leader.

* * *

Something to realize about leadership is that when you're under any type of pressure, stress, or uncertainty, or in over your head as a leader, it shows on your face, it shows in your voice, it shows in your walk. It's on display to everyone, and no matter how hard you try to hide it, you can't. People are watching you.

One thing I learned as a leader when I made it to the executive level is someone is always watching you. Not in a creepy sort of way, but watching you to figure out if they should use you as their leadership role model, looking at you to decide if they can actually make it in this organization, looking at you to decide if they want to be a leader themselves. For myriad reasons, people will be watching you as the leader. Some watch you just to see if you're going to crack—if you're able to actually lead. If you go into a position realizing that you're being watched, that you're always on stage as a leader, you must know whatever you wear on your face will get transmitted and passed along to your people.

When I would come into the office, people were watching to see what kind of day I was having. They're watching to see how I was moving. Okay, is he in a good mood? Is he in a bad mood? Even when I would come out of meetings with my then leaders or then peers, they were watching to see my demeanor coming out of the meeting. Is he pissed off? Is he happy? Is he excited? Is he nervous? I realized, probably a little too late, I was on display. I was the biggest billboard to my direct reports. I was the barometer—and I didn't know it. Many times, they'd fashion their day, their night, their week, if you will, around how I showed up on a Monday morning, first thing, walking into the office, on a Tuesday afternoon after the last meeting of the day, or any of those things, after a town hall meeting. All of those experiences helped me to realize that though you many not say anything, when you're stressed out, all your people know it. The best way to defuse this is to say, "Hey, I've got a lot going on right now. Just wanted to let you know I am working through them and processing some things." Just be honest with people. Most people get it. But when you tell everybody you are fine, and your body language looks everything but fine, you start to lose credibility as a leader. You can't afford to do that.

KEYS TO UNLOCK THE DOOR TO EFFECTIVE LEADERSHIP

9) Don't Be One to Talk a Good Game --- Sometimes what's not there is more important than what is. If you show your lack of substance what kind of signal does that send? Leadership is more than sound-bites and hyperbole. Talking a good game does not get you far when it comes to creating and developing a better self, a better colleague and peer, and the people that do much of the real work that makes organizations successful. When all you are is "talk" you have failed to open the hearts and minds of those you are supposed to lead. Deeds not words should be your guiding mantra.

10) Don't Play the Blame Game --- The blame game is not one you should sit in on. In life and business there are always things that will go wrong. In large organizations (as with government) you can surely bet that somewhere, somehow, someone is screwing up... and you may be part of having to deal with it. It's okay to identify the cause but don't spend time on blame, get quickly on to working the problem to come up with a solution. Blame is not how problems and issues are resolved.

11) Accept Change as Frequent Visitor --- along with the fact that there are always problems and issues to deal with, is that change is constant. In dealing with change you can make mistakes and these are often caused by internal politics, generational differences and miscommunication. That last item also holds the key to minimizing and mitigating missteps—leaders must communicate clearly when it comes to expectations and execution of policies within the organization.

12) Conduct Stay Interviews Often --- Understand why people want to stay with your company rather than fixate on why some chooses to go. This ties back to the impact the leader and/or organization makes at the granular, employee, level. Odds are if it's unfavorable... then at some point that person is going to leave and not many (if any) of their answers will be of importance. Leaders and organizations are better served if they try to find out what makes people enjoy working for them or for the company. It's a reinforcement of the positives that eliminates the need for retroactive fixes of someone's perceived negatives regarding a leader or company and in the long run... this proves to be far more important.

CHAPTER FOUR

The Importance of Context and Rationality

"Success is to be measured not so much by the position that one has reached in life as by the obstacles which he has overcome."

—Booker T. Washington

Remembering what's Important

That First Day of Work (ever in your life)

Remember that feeling on your first day of work. Not your first day of your current job, but your first day of work ever. For me it was an up swelling of pride and independence. It was also nerves and anxiety, but eventually all of that settled down and I got into a rhythm. I learned a lot in that first job. I learned about the value of hard work, I learned that time equals money and most importantly I learned that in work, as in life, you have to earn what you get. At least for us common folk.

I had a boss who cared for me and yet he challenged me. He pushed me at times, but at the end of the day I was rewarded in so many ways. That job built a foundation for me. It provided me with a toolkit for how to work. I was young, but could be stubborn, and that job taught me about humility. It was one of the best lessons I've ever had. I've tried to remain humble ever since. Confident, but unpretentious. I feel like there's nothing I can't accomplish, but I don't need to brag to the world about it.

As you reflect on your first job, think about how you felt and what you learned. Do you still draw on that today? Have you passed those values and lessons on? Have you thought about how you can build an experience for you and your people that brings back those initial feelings of excitement, pride and independence? If you're feeling stuck in the middle and you feel like there's no place for you to go, I challenge you to reshape your role, your environment and your behaviors. The most important thing you can do is to find that feeling of independence. Then figure out a way to feel passionate again about what you do.

Understand there's no secret sauce, no remedy that works for everyone no matter who they are or their circumstances. You need to find what works specific to you. Life's too short to feel stuck. How you get unstuck is based on how motivated you are for that challenge. Remember your early lessons, time is money, you earn your keep and you earn what's coming to you. Even if the odds feel stacked against you, it's on you to make the shift.

Performance Review Reality Check

Which side of the bell curve did you land on this year? How did that conversation go for you? Did you buy it? Most don't, and for good reason; it's broken. The system doesn't work and everyone knows it's a joke, but we all keep marching in line.

Even if you landed on the upside of the performance bell curve this year, do you feel good about it? Beyond the larger bonus or the merit increase, how do you feel? How do you feel knowing that to get that spiff, it came at the expense of someone else? You worked hard, and yes you earned it, but that's not the point. The point is that you have friends who have worked just as hard, and they were given a sucker punch to the ego.

Here's how I've heard it, "Well, you had a good year. You know we had to trim the so-called 'fat' this year. So it was only the good ones left. It's why you're still here. But, you also know that we're only allowed to give a certain number of "exceeds expectation" ratings. And, well, you were placed into achieves this year. But, I really want you to know that I think you're doing great work. To be honest, we don't really give out exceeds. I've only seen it done on a few occasions, so keep up the good work."

Inspirational isn't it?

Hardly the practice of Employee Engagement that many describe as best practice. I can't tell you how many employees I've heard from about how demotivating this message is to them both personally and professionally. Would you go to war with or for a boss like that? Do you really feel appreciated by your company when you hear that? Even on the upside of the conversation, you have to be thinking about all of the support from the 'achieves' group that got you where you are. We're not in this alone, and yet we have a system that is designed to undermine the most valuable asset available—relationships.

If you run the numbers (and I have in the past for more than one organization) you might be surprised to find that the higher you get to in the organization, the higher the average yearly rating employees receive. Why is that? Because the "fat" has been trimmed? Why, because only the cream rises to the top? I don't buy that... especially since I've had to sell it before in my career. It's time to get real. Let's put a system in place that we can all march behind, and feel good about the cadence being called. Forward, march!

Up the Ladders to the Kids Table

Have you ever sat at "the kids table" for holiday meals with your extended family? If you did, you'll certainly remember what it was like when you finally "graduated" to the "grownups" table. Keep this in mind.

As I found myself moving farther up the corporate ladder, you would think that leading would be the skill I would be measured on most often. But in "Executive Land", it can be difficult to find that right mix of delivery, of owning things—not only from a tactical standpoint but from a strategic one as well. I think many of my Gen X counterparts struggle with that as well, because we have Baby Boomer bosses, who do not believe we should be where we are, yet.

They still see you as a kid, and say, "Okay, kid, go work on this." They don't welcome us at the strategy table yet because they don't believe our "youthful" career trajectory allows us to be there to share in the strategic thought generation. That's probably one of the biggest mistakes the Baby Boomer leaders make; thinking only their generation has any strategic thinking to add to the discussion.

That's a very candid statement about what I've experienced in "Executive Land." You almost have to become a different person to be an executive. For some Gen Xers, that process doesn't really fit them. It's hard to turn off who you are each day, or not be the person you have been up to this point in life just for the sake of making a certain amount of money or to have a certain title.

Unfortunately, that's going to come back to bite a lot of people in the pants. My generation of colleagues realizes the fact that we're worth a lot more than we're getting credit for, and we're stuck between two generations and trying to prove ourselves to both (to be listened to by Boomers and to lead Millennials and Gen Yers).

How do you remain visible in a place where many would rather you be invisible? There is much value Gen Xers could add, more that we can do, but many of us are not getting a chance to make those contributions. Those valid feelings of being undervalued, underestimated, and marginalized contribute to the purported "Generation X malaise".

Changing Workforce... Changing Business Climate

Take the dynamics of a changing workforce and an evolving business climate and ask yourself; is there enough talent out there to move your organization forward? Are you positioned well enough to get the talent that you need? Suspend for a moment the thought that I'm talking about A-list talent, and ask yourself if there is enough talent in general to sustain your organization.

Today the answer is very likely yes. But I would venture that is in large part due to the economy and the fact that Boomers aren't quite leaving at the rate we expected, and unemployment is high enough that people are legitimately scared to go elsewhere. Lastly, people that are unemployed are willing to take any old job. But it will not stay this way and there are signs that a recovery is well underway. Things change, and although this may take more time than most other changes, you should start to plan for the potential shortages of talent in your organization.

It's a problem. Not an emergency quite yet, but it should be on your radar. Your organization should have a plan for how to manage this in the foreseeable future. Unemployment rates of recent college graduates are troubling. Recent graduates have traditionally been able to take time to learn on the job, working under the protection of more seasoned employees. But as things turn around and Boomers leave, these unemployed will be asked to jump right into the organization, and they won't have the benefit of time. They'll be asked to fill a fairly significant void in the organization.

So, the question becomes, what will you do to prepare for this? Do you have a development group? Are they even aware of this as a pending issue? Have you started to think this one through?

From the Frontline in the War on Talent

We keep hearing about this global war for talent, and for good reason; it's about to get real. The world continues to shrink, technology continues to alter traditional patterns of work and knowledge continues to reign supreme. Compound all of this with more and more Boomers readying to leave the workplace and the war for talent just got very serious.

This is your chance to step up as a leader and ensure that knowledge and skills are transferred successfully and the next generation of workers is ready to carry the torch. You can help the process along by evaluating your current talent management process.

Start by asking what the critical roles in the organization are. Who holds them and have the right successors been identified to fill the critical roles. Is the 'bench' ready now, or do they need more development, more seasoning? While you are at it, ask yourself this...where are you on the bench; on or off?

Once you identify those roles and the succession plan, you need to start thinking three steps ahead and determine how those roles and skills are going to change in the highly co-related and integrated world we now operate in. Are you prepared to go to war? You'll need new talent, fresh ideas, and new insights because without it, your battleship will sink and you could lose the game (or the war).

Take it one step further: does your bench strength run deep enough into your organization? You may have your 'ready now' successors that can jump in an instant. While their waiting for their turn or chance... recall these high potentials (and they must be or they wouldn't be in your line of succession) are more likely to leave than any of your other employees. Because they have options. They have networks, and even in tough times, they're still moving. And if you're not moving them, they will find ways to move themselves; even if it's out of your sphere of benefit.

The war on talent is real, and it's officially here, so rise up and get ready to rumble. It's your turn now.

100 Years of Talent Management

Over the last one hundred years, the economy has gone through several stages in which success has been defined differently. Each stage has had its own structure, governing patterns, roles, talent practices and assumptions about people.

The Industrial Age was when the economy was manufacturing-oriented. A few people made decisions, command and control was vital and employees were like replaceable machine parts—something considered a cost to be controlled. The Knowledge Age developed as the economy became more service-oriented. Decision-making was pushed down to more people. The 'knowledge worker' phrase was coined and people were viewed as potential assets.

In the Global Talent Age, success is defined differently. To be successful organizations must innovate, be agile, respond to change quickly and encourage creativity. Organizations are no longer huge and monolithic, but rather consist of value chains of various companies and suppliers often in different countries. In this age the 'right talent," and not 'all employees,' is the most valued asset.

This provides an example of different skills being important in different eras. In the industrial age, it was all about economies of scale, efficiency and control. Because this defined economic success, it was what managers were expected to do. As the economy moved to the service sector, success meant something different; and managers had to adapt and adjust.

In the Talent Age success is characterized by innovation, agility and speed of choice; all of which are highly talent-dependent. The manager needs to become a talent leader to unleash and leverage the capabilities of people. And to do that, leaders need to also become experts at workforce planning. Something that is a very underdeveloped practice in most Talent Age organizations. This stems from the fact that talent management has not been viewed as a strategic process but rather as people practices that are administrative and operational in nature. This is a dangerous perspective carried over from the Industrial Age. Most businesses have no talent plans at all and will therefore be affected greatly by retirements, downsizing and other external and internal factors.

One of the most difficult aspects of workforce planning is predicting future skills needed, not just extrapolating current skills into the future. This is part of the art of workforce planning. But there is great opportunity for organizations to do workforce planning right and for it to make a vital difference in effective leadership for the present and future success of the organization.

Talent Management Perfected at Southwest

Success stories are useful ways to examine the role that talent management can play in the growth and development of an organization. Southwest Airlines is the largest domestic air carrier in the United States. It is also the only one that is, and has been, consistently profitable for a number of years.

Its success has been determined by a number of factors.

1. A clear and consistent strategy of democratizing the sky and travel for a low-cost
2. Some key operational choices early in the airline's development that allowed it to prosper, even if against conventional wisdom: No hubs, one type of airplane and going into cheaper airports within big city regions.
3. Some good decisions that impact operations in a real-time manner and
4. Their talent strategy that puts employees first.

Southwest Airlines has built a powerful talent brand and every year there are over 100,000 applicants for about 5,000 jobs—so it's harder to get a job at Southwest Airlines than to get into Harvard. Others have tried (and failed) to emulate the Southwest talent culture because of its role in the overall success of the airline. Success that I enjoy personally as a customer. For years now, my first choice for air travel is always Southwest Airlines.

This story shows that there are several reasons for success, not just talent management; but that, unlike gambles on the price of oil; talent is always a lever that can be developed and improved. Talent practices and integrated talent management are important today because they address vital strategic and organizational issues. It is not because these are HR or training priorities; it is because they directly impact intangible assets and an organization's ability to compete.

For boards and CEOs the driver of mitigating risk through stronger talent pipelines is close behind productivity improvement (and in some cases is the number one driver). Organizations are stuck if leadership doesn't recognize their organization's most critical roles, or have a talent pool ready to fill openings internally as they happen. Promoting from within produces cost savings that are real, tangible and have a direct impact on effective talent management. The most obvious case is the money lost when valuable and talented employees leave an organization—unwanted turnover is more about talent mismanagement than talent management. Integrated talent management, if practiced as a priority, is the best method in aligning the organization to better execute on its strategy.

NFL Draft: Talent Management Takes the Stage

Talent scouts and evaluators for every NFL team are looking for that hidden gem. We already know about the high profile guys, and we probably know more about them than necessary, but it's the late round guys, the grinders, who really fill out a team. This is where you build your bench strength. They may not be ready now to start, but if you give them a year or two of seasoning, they may shine for your team for years to come.

Look at some of the more notable, successful quarterbacks, not late round guys, but they were athletes whose stock dropped quickly in round one of the draft. One in particular was in contention for the number one pick leading up to the draft and he slid late into round one, where a team grabbed him. They let him sit for a few years, asked him to learn and soak in everything he could, and now look at him, he's one of the best quarterbacks in the league.

My point is, someone believed in him. They knew they could grow him into an elite quarterback and they were willing to let a franchise QB go when the time was right for that quarterback to step into the starting job. It goes back to my principles of know, show, grow and flow. If you can get this sequence down with your talent, you'll be able to keep a well-stocked bench ready to perform.

But I digress. What really impresses me about the draft is the processes that teams have in place to scout and evaluate their players. It goes beyond the physical dimensions of football and looks at the emotional, intellectual and character traits of players. If you have dirty laundry and are about to enter the NFL, it's getting aired out. The thoroughness of the silent process is astounding. Granted your organization may not have the resources that some of these teams do, but you would do well to think about how their process may align with your culture and what may work for you.

To me, the most revealing aspect of the draft is how the good teams rely on it to build their strength from within. What I mean is, look at some of the other recently successful championship teams in the NFL. They went external to the free agent market to bring in high priced players who were supposed to bring a Super Bowl victory to the team. Only it didn't work. The team that did ultimately win the title actually lost two of its key free agents brought in one veteran center and re-signed a reserve guard. Their fan base and the media went ballistic at what they thought was poor management while their rivals supposedly stocked up and created the Dream Team. The team found their grinders. These were the guys that the organization knew could grow and flow into playing time, and it worked. When guys got injured they stepped up.

Take some time to think about your talent process, what does you 'draft' look like? Are you always chasing the high-priced external talent? Or are you growing your people and getting them ready to play in the big game when your team needs them the most?

Rationality, Relevance and the Real Importance of Experience

Is Your Organization Rational

Is your organization rational? Think twice before you answer this one, in some ways it's a trick question. Before I go any further, I should define what I mean by rational. In its most basic sense, a rational organization has a formalized structure, a clear sense of organizational goals, rules and behaviors that are highly structured, and cooperation is both deliberate and conscious. If you were to break this out and look at each component independently, how would you answer this question?

Now, think for a moment about your answer.

Do you have clear organizational goals that can be described across the enterprise? Do people act deliberate, based on formalized rules? Regardless of how you answer this question, I think the more important question is SHOULD your organization be rational? Is it an appropriate model of organizations in the current workforce environment? Is it realistic to think that people A) are rational actors themselves and B) are not a part of a larger ecosystem that influences decisions, thoughts, behaviors and interactions?

If you are part of a rational organization (and here is the twist... most of us are), are you effectively able to respond to the world around you? Are you building structures and systems that enable customers, suppliers and employees to make decisions that are fast, flexible and adaptable? Are your systems designed to not leave your employees stuck with the noise and confusion in the middle between the work you ask them to do, and having a true understanding of what they need to do in order to grow in your organization? Do you need to open up your structure to accommodate the new realities to today's globally competitive environment we are dealing with? And if so, how would you go about making the needed changes? The answer to the question for every organization is dependent on what you are trying to accomplish and who your competitors are, but that is up to you to figure out as the first step.

Being rational sounds like a good idea, but the reality is much different. We are not rational beings (see *Predictably Irrational* by Dan Ariely) and can predict how irrational we are. But our motives and behaviors are not simply subject to one defined set of rules, and as a result, our actions are not always so clearly determined. Add on a layer of complexity about how we interact in a fast paced, ever changing environment and all bets are off.

One Sentence... and Only One

If I gave you one sentence to describe your organization, which words would you choose? Could you do it? Would they resonate with the employee base? How about with your leadership team? Do you think your competitors and your customers would agree?

I have worked in many organizations where they were wearing blinders about the importance of identity and how the absence of honest character at the organizational core defined them. The internal talk was great, but it's a problem when you literally have to create talking points for your employees to use when they are at parties, or out in the community to describe and defend the company. Seriously, I am not making this up. In one organization, employees were even mailed cards on a quarterly basis to hand out to friends or family members who had issues with their customer service. I would hear people say our name on the train, or in an airport, and you could literally hear the condescension in their voice. It is a shame too, because it was and is actually a great product, and there are a lot of great people in the company. They had an identity and company character problem... and when you can't pinpoint identity and establish the integrity that tends to mean you develop a relevancy problem. And over time that can and will kill a business.

I do not mean to pick on this one company, this happens in all industries and so many companies struggle with their internal and external brand. They have illusions of grandeur. Just look at the Wall Street firms and all of the issues they have.

I know a lot of good people in the financial sector. If you asked them, they would not put hubris or greed as one of the three words to describe their company, but 90% of the general population probably would. Trust has been squandered. It is a tough time for many of our established companies. They are feeling the winds of change grow to hurricane strength. They are deeply entrenched and positioned; it has been a long haul for many of them.

The reality is it is not going to get easier. Competition continues to increase; new ventures are more nimble and exciting for many people. This puts even greater pressure on our roles as strategic HR partners. We need to help build an employee value proposition that resonates internally and externally—that radiates relevancy to the market (clients, customers, consumers and investors). We also need to help ensure that the words used internally are reinforced in our interactions with external audiences.

Finally, it's our responsibility to take senior leaders to task to implement the structures and the culture that will enable the internal talk to become the external reality. A company or a culture is not innovative just by saying so. It is the role of senior leaders to make it so. They must grow and nourish a culture that supports true innovation. Senior leaders must be out front; describing the organization in just one sentence... and hopefully, with the same positive words.

It Is About Real Experiences, Not Training Programs

What's the culture of development like at your office? Do you put a heavy emphasis on training, or do you focus your efforts on real experiences? If you're really looking to make an impact you should be focusing on experiences. According to the Center for Creative Leadership, talent development activities align to a 70-20-10 rule.

What that means is:

- 70% of learning in your organization takes place on the job through challenging assignments and projects.
- 20% of learning comes from your peer network (could be mentors, managers, friends, etc.)
- 10% of learning actually comes from training programs.

Think about this for a minute, if you're putting enormous efforts into building training programs, are you really getting a return on your investment? Probably not, unless you've built real world experiences into your program.

In a former organization where I worked, there were ten competencies, six behavioral traits, nine characteristics of successful leadership and hundreds of training opportunities, all supposedly aligned. Our brains can't handle all of that... nor should we force it to try.

Make it simple. Make it about the experiences they need to be successful, and your people will thank you for it.

If you want your people to develop: build experiences, challenge them, and line them up for success. You want to talk about talent management: strip it down and make it easy for your people to understand...it's the experience that matters most. So start thinking simply. Think about Apple...the world's most renowned company; simple is elegant. It's not easy to get to simple. But here are some tips to help:

1. Identify your critical roles
2. Identify the experiences that are needed to be in that role
3. Simplify your competency structure- focus on 3 to 5 max
4. Make your competencies progressive
5. Make your competencies align to the critical experiences
6. Align your training efforts to the competencies and include experiences
7. Help managers build experiences into employee's work
8. Reduce the noise

Why What You Can Do Is More Important Than What You Can "Sell"

There is an initial transaction between someone applying for a position and their prospective employer, the company looking to fill a position. It involves something that many Gen Xers are uncomfortable with but exists in the job market — and in their career climb. It is the need to know how to position and present yourself, or sell yourself. This is especially important today even as we start to see recovery in our recession-wracked business environment.

The best way to sell yourself is by being prepared and, in many ways by doing this; it does the selling for you. It's self-promotion by preparation. And by doing it you start down a path to leading toward what you want. This simple effort separates the men from the boys and the women from the girls.

If you know the role you want, and you've looked at all that you have to do, or the experiences you need to have, and said, "That's too hard., "It will take too long." Or "I don't want to do it." You just learned everything you need to know about yourself (say, "thanks" for not having to pay for a psych evaluation or a counselor to help you figure things out). You now know that you really don't want it bad enough. You want the trappings, you want the rewards, you want the glory, but you aren't prepared to do the work it takes to get there. And you know what? That's not a comfortable conversation for someone to have with themselves, but it's one of the most necessary conversations you will ever have in your career.

It's easier to get somewhere in life and career if you are brutally honest enough to understand who and where you are from the beginning. If you don't feel like you're ready or don't want to do all it takes to reach your aspirations, then don't do it. But more importantly, don't whine, cry, and moan to all who will listen when you don't get to that level. Especially if you know deep down in your heart that you haven't done everything or are not willing to do everything it takes to succeed.

To reach executive management, we're not simply talking about entering a popularity contest. Yes, popularity and professional brand are important, but at the end of the day, it all boils down to the resume you place in front of the hiring manager and how you come across as the embodiment of what is on paper.

One goal I have for myself that I will share with you is this: I've always set myself up so whenever my resume is put in the hands of a decision maker, for the position I know I am ready for, I never want them to think, "This guy would be perfect for us if he only had _____."

I've been obsessive in taking care so that never happens. There is no "if only he had" to be found in reading my resume. Perhaps that strategy could work for you, too. Ask for feedback on your resume from others; address any misses they find in your resume by filling them with either new experiences or learning where appropriate.

I don't believe you can be overqualified. Overqualified is not in my vocabulary. I prefer highly qualified. Highly qualified says I am versatile and have many transferable skills, whereas overqualified says I am at the end of the line in one job or career field.

I studied my resume long and hard, and then, I went shopping. I went online and found job descriptions for the roles I would want to have, and printed out the job descriptions. Everything I saw as a required or a recommended skill in those job descriptions, I put on a qualifications shopping list. When I had a full list of what I felt I needed, I went about getting those experiences, the correct level of education, and the most contemporary certifications. What do I need to have on my resume that is currently missing but is recommended or needed for the role I'm looking for with a good company? Better yet, what things should be on my resume that will make them think, "We have to talk to this this guy! His background and experience is perfect."

I have worked in multiple industries at increasing levels of accountability and seniority, building my career step-by-step. I have been an entrepreneur and have built and sold a business. I have a doctorate in education, have worked for international companies and am certified in HR and project management. I have been a Vice President and am a military veteran. I have an interesting story to tell and I am good at connecting with people, which in my opinion is the quintessential skill of an effective leader.

In short, I worked hard to make myself into the perfect candidate. It's taken sacrifice, time, and plenty of money to be able to do that, but I believe that if you're going to compete for the top positions, you've got to be exemplary, you've got to be extraordinary, and a lot of hard work goes into that. This is not only required in establishing the strength of the resume and credentials but also in networking to make the right contacts that will help you in your career. I never lost sight of the fact that the resume I built was only to get me the interview. It was up to me, once I am in the interview, to sell myself so well that I got the job. And I have been successful—and smart enough to never turn down a job interview and wise enough to not accept every job offer.

People Who Need People

Perhaps the single most important element of any business operations: organizations need people. They must hire and retain people to innovate and create new products and services and to support existing products and services so they can continue to increase profits and preserve their company's growth.

The challenge for us as emerging Generation X leaders is to do more with less—in this case, fewer people—and we must inspire a workforce with different generational values. To be successful as 21st century leaders, we must guide our fewer in number Generation X peers and the newly emerging Generation Y employees through difficult business challenges such as smoothing the loss of the technical knowledge and skills of the retiring Baby Boomer workforce. We must have the leadership ability to align generational peers and inspire Generation Y. Our vision for new managers must set a clear direction to maintain productivity from a workforce with fewer skills. To further complicate the challenge, we must deal with the mismanagement of our government and other governments, by ill-advised policies about energy, environments, intellectual property, and trade. Future leaders must adjust to the global markets and currencies variation from the newly formed economic partnerships. As leaders we must develop and then preserve a global competitive edge within our industry to ensure the future of our organizations.

Over the next five to ten years, most of the Baby Boomers will retire and leave their careers behind. The baby boom began in the mid-1940s and ended in the mid-1960s. Baby Boomers are sons and daughters of the Silent Generation, the Veterans, and the Builders. This generation of men and women knew sacrifice, discipline, common value, teamwork, and strength. Baby Boomers, as they merged into the workforce, brought a skilled, driven, and team-orientated attitude into work that complemented their parents. The Baby Boomers unprecedented work ethic and innovation drove major business growth within the United States. As they retire, they will leave a void within the workforce. This void is a large burden on us, the emerging Generation X leaders because we are losing senior managers, technical workers, and knowledge keepers that built the current state of our companies. As these workers retire in large numbers, are we ready now or will we be ready soon to replace them?

The Looming Challenge

There are a lot of unhappy Gen Xers out there who are not making the money they need to live the life they want to live, should live, or feel they could live—because they're stuck in the middle. I think that's one of the hardest pills to swallow; the realization that we seek career happiness, and work life balance while quickly coming to the conclusion we may not be able to simultaneously pay our bills and have the career that would truly make us happy.

Some have traded career happiness for money to be able to live a better life, but are instead slowly living a life much like our Baby Boomer coworkers and bosses. It's an interesting juxtaposition in the form of a steep climb of the personal career decision tree with branches so twisted that it is hard to determine which limb to choose next that will allow us to reach the blue sky.

As a Gen Xer, the sad truth is that you've got to do your time or prove yourself in the company before you're taken seriously or for the Baby Boomers to see you as the executive you know yourself to be capable of becoming. Everyone will tell you that there's no greater way to prove yourself in any company than to deliver well on products with consistency.

Proving yourself as an executive in every company is different. Some organizations want you to deliver on creating a strategy to save money or make money. Others will say you must deliver by adding to the value of the company. Still others will expect you to exhibit "strategic thinking and tactical doing". Some still might believe that delivering on mundane administrative task defines being an effective leader or manager.

Those latter are two distinctly different things though they are often lumped together. I believe you lead people but you manage projects. As a corporate executive, I didn't manage my people; I led them and allowed them to amaze me with their talent. One of my favorite things to say to my direct reports was:

*"I'll share with you the what, why, and when for every task...
You get to amaze me with the how it gets done."*

I don't like to tell people how to do their job because I don't like people telling me how to do my job. If you hire someone to tell them how to do their job, why don't you just do the job yourself and save someone the misery of micromanagement. So instead, I would tell them what they needed to do and allowed them to use their creativity, their intellect, their professionalism, and their expertise to come back with an innovative solution to meet the need as identified.

And this one statement to them did one more thing. It empowered them in their work and by giving them that it allowed me to work with, and lead versus manage, some of the smartest people, and hardest working professionals in the current workforce. In the end, this way of thinking and acting was seen by many of my past direct reports as the hallmark of a true manager of talent... and a truly talented manager.

Perceptions and Performance

Years ago, there was a study done in the world of education that looked at teacher perceptions and student performance. At a high level, the report showed a strong correlation between perception and performance. When teachers were primed in advance about how their students would perform (regardless of evidence/data) they tended to believe in what they heard, and in turn, the students tended to perform up to the level of expectations the teachers had for them. What was interesting is that researchers intentionally flipped the script. They took the lower performing students and they talked them up and said how great they would be in the classroom next year. The teachers that were primed for them to be great actually showed huge improvements in performance with the students' year over year.

A new study was released about student perceptions of self and how they perform. Interestingly, in the United States students were pretty consistent in rating themselves. If they said they were good at math, the evidence tended to hold true. However, when researchers went internationally, the results changed. Students didn't report themselves in the same vein as their American peers. They tended to rate themselves lower than their American counterparts. The research is tricky here. It's not that Americans are pounding their chests. Rather, it's that in the global pool, participants tended to rate themselves against higher standards. They perceive their level of achievement differently than that of their American counterparts.

So, what does this have to do with me, you and becoming more effective leaders? It's about perceptions and performance. Imagine if we believed in our employees to do exceptional work. Imagine if we stopped hearing about the talent shortage (guilty) and stopped saying how unprepared the next generation is to work in this environment. Imagine if we actually believed that they could live up to the hype. If we tamped down the anxiety about not being prepared for the next phase of business we may actually see a world where people step up and outperform our expectations. Sometimes all it takes is a little belief... and effective leadership.

The Wave of Coming Retirements

Engage Your Boomers

There's a lot of talk about how to engage Millennials and Gen Xers out there, but little is being said about how to engage an aging workforce and the Boomers. They are at the sunset of their careers, which actually makes their level of engagement even more important. It's interesting to me that we don't talk about this often, perhaps it's because we think they're set in their ways and ready to ride out their glory years.

In fact, that's not true. Boomer managers and leaders are at the stage in their career where they're thinking about the legacy they will leave behind, the challenges they overcame and the success they accomplished. It may not be easy, but it's the right time to tap into this and use it to your company's advantage. You can take some fairly simple steps to make this happen:

1. Set up a coaching community for High-Potentials
2. Create rotational assignments
3. Build a knowledge sharing platform
4. Establish mentoring programs

You can appeal to ego and let them know they will indeed leave behind a legacy, that the torch needs to be passed and you're asking them to rise to one more challenge before they go. The coaching community would provide Boomers with the opportunity to work with high potential future leaders. You can structure it so that they are able to provide on the ground advice and consultation. If done right, it can even be an avenue for them to stay on with the organization after retirement in some nonemployee capacity. For the rotational program, you should find younger employees who have the ability and aspiration for broader roles and move them under Boomers for short periods of time. The knowledge sharing platform is a way to capture the knowledge that your Boomers have and it enables them to continue to support and grow the company's legacy and culture. Lastly, you can create a formal mentoring program open to all employees that enable the Boomers to share their wisdom while simultaneously learning from others. Even in their twilight years, engaging your Boomers is a critical people strategy that can lead to long-term success.

Building the Replacements

I had the opportunity to recently see a High-Potential program in action and I took note of the palpable excitement among the group. What I also noticed was that the company didn't shy away from telling these participants why they were there and how important they were to the organization. And while there were no guarantees made to the participants, their expectations of promotion, and success were set. "You're the future leaders of this organization."

Dollars and time were invested heavily into this program and make no mistake there was a clear message to the participants that they should cherish the investment and seize upon it to help them get to the next level. There's no guarantee they'll get to that level, but what struck me most was how invested the company was in setting them up for success. Based on what I saw, the investment made was more than just dollars. The leadership team made it a point to be present, supportive and fully committed with their time, resources and knowledge.

This program has built up a base of support, by convincing leaders that this was the right next step. From what I heard, these leaders fully back the program. But as we all know, time is fleeting, so to keep the leaders engaged, this program will need to continue its momentum and build its legacy by showing its long-term impact. Leaders won't stay onboard forever; you have to figure out how to keep them supportive.

So, I ask you, how invested is your leadership in developing your organization's next round of great leaders? Are they stuck in the middle between writing a check and making a real commitment of their time? Because in this economic environment, time is more valuable than money with regard to investing in your leaders of the future.

* * *

Being rational really means selling what you can do and following it up by delivering. A lot of people out there will tell you the whole idea about being a leader is do as I say, not as I do. Or do as I do, not as I say. I think it's both. We leaders get so trapped into thinking we need to always win, always be successful, always know the answer to every question, always be a fountain of wisdom, always be in a position where we're doing well. I believe the harder you try to be flawless, the more flaws you're going to exhibit.

One of the biggest flaws people have is to overpromise and under deliver. Nothing goes worse for you as a leader than what happens when you under deliver. Because that means your word is no good. It means you have bitten off more than you can chew. It's much better to under promise and over deliver. Sometimes instead of a massive high-visibility project, it's almost better to have one or two small things that you're working on—and then succeed at those. Get the wins. Get the Ws. Get people to see you said you were going to do something and you've done it. It doesn't matter if it's something small. Just achieve it. Then you move on to the next thing. You start to build a track record of delivering, of being a person of your word. That goes a very long way. A lot farther than many people realize. People want to follow a leader who can roll up their sleeves and get things done, and follow through when they say they're going to do something.

* * *

My time in the Navy time taught me that your first week onboard ship will tell you all that you need to know about that ship—and indirectly, its commanding officer and leadership chain. It's much like that in private organizations, too. You have to become familiar with the people and believe them to be who they show themselves to be. Allow them to show you who and what and how the organization really is. In doing so, you set yourself up to lead within the context of that organization. What I mean by that is there are many different leadership styles. I mentioned I am a big fan of situational leadership. But strategy, leadership models, leadership philosophies, all those things take a bow to culture.

Taking a look at the culture you are coming into will help you realize whether or not your natural leadership style will be effective. Compare that to what type of leader the organization holds up as the best it has to offer. When you can figure out who an organization would claim as some of its best leaders, the best thing I would say to you is take that opportunity and figure out how you can emulate those leaders. Try to get yourself in a position where you can find out from that leader how they got to that place? How did they go about leading within the context of their organization? A good way to do this is if you're a peer of that individual is to say to them. "I'm just coming onboard. I would love to grab lunch or coffee." And when you do, ask him or her, "You've been here a while and I'm just coming in. What type of leadership model or leadership style works best here? How have you gotten your leadership perspective to be so adopted or so effective?" Listen to what he or she has to say. Take it in for consideration and make that your next target to create growth opportunity for yourself—take the leadership style that you bring to the table and mold to fit within the culture you just joined.

KEYS TO UNLOCK THE DOOR TO EFFECTIVE LEADERSHIP

13) Think Thrice, Question Twice, Act Once --- How we feel about much, if not everything, in life is based on context and relevancy. These two things are important aspects of effective leadership. Make how you lead consistently and contextually relevant and you will be the type of leader needed by both those you lead and for your organization. Think about what is the right thing to do given all the data, the people, circumstances and situation. Don't make a knee-jerk decision based on your own perception—look hard at, measure and consider all the factors so you make a better decision.

14) Seek Clarity over Assumption --- You also have to be rational and rationality only comes with clarity as to who you are as a person and organization. The problem is that human beings, even with the best intentions, are often irrational. So you have to be aware of any unreasonableness that creeps in. Weigh things and see how they balance out... don't presuppose a decision... apply calm thought to all aspects of life and business and that will cool down the heat and lower the pressure to make a quick, and probably flawed, decision.

15) Make Professional Development a Contact Sport --- Education is good. Training is good. Real world experience is better. When developing yourself and/or your organization—look to the benefits that come from actual work in the field—getting your hands dirty— seeing what it's like in the trenches. You'll come away a stronger leader and will build a more effective and productive work force with that understanding. What you (and your people) can actually do is much more important than any other aspect of business.

16) Manage the Process, By Leading The People --- It's the people. Without them what is a leader... what is an organization? And it's a fact that leaders in the 21st century are faced with many challenges that previous generations never had to face: expanding global competition, a surge in loss of intellectual resources with the wave of coming Boomer retirements and a work force with different generational values. To lead effectively you have to understand those you lead. You have to know their capabilities and address their concerns. Make those two action items the center of your preparation as a leader. Seek to influence and inspire, not to drive and direct.

CHAPTER FIVE

Presentation Meets Perception

Tone, Tenor and Seeing Shadows

"Men make history, and not the other way around. In periods where there is no leadership, society stands still. Progress occurs when courageous, skillful leaders seize the opportunity to change things for the better. "

—Harry S. Truman

Words Must Be More than Wind

If you lead people, learn to lead by your actions not your words. As they say in *The Game of Thrones* on HBO, *words are wind*. If you are leading people and not setting standards through your actions, you are missing an opportunity to inspire your people. Too many times in my career I have personally encountered and heard, from others, stories of leaders who talk to hear themselves talk. They are in love with their own echo.

Unfortunately, this extends to how they lead their people. They think that as leader their primary task is to find ways to critique their employees—letting their voice ring. Now, do not misconstrue what I'm saying here. Providing feedback is critical in any organization. However, it's the WAY in which these leaders give it that tells the tale. Vocal leaders search for anything they can use as a critique of their employees and go above and beyond to find the words to describe faults. But it's very rare they find the right words to praise. They grasp for things. And the easiest thing at hand, for them, is criticism; thinking that will turn them around... after all, I'm their boss. And that is the shallowest form of leadership.

It may sound like the devil is in the details—what to say and how to say it, or that leadership is merely accomplished by having an executive presence that evenhandedly communicates to all within the organization—I'm not saying it isn't important, it undoubtedly is. But it's one part of being a good leader. If you are a one-way type; always talking and never listening, ultimately your people have to (and will) consider the source and begin to discount the importance. It is hard to take feedback seriously from a leader who cannot listen. It is even more difficult when you watch as that leader, intent on having their say, ignores details you consider critical to the success of what you do.

Words are wind. But they swirl and carry many things to many ears and talking too much lowers interest in listening—your words become a cheap commodity. Wrong things said and right things not done can sink a career and damage a business. So as a leader, be careful what you say and pay more attention to how you act. Learn to inspire with what you do... not what you say. Words must be more than just wind.

Patterns of Interaction

How often do you communicate with your team? How about with key stakeholders cross-functionally? Are there people in either of those groups that you don't talk with on a regular basis? Do they know it? Are they aware they are on the outside?

If you are unsure and cannot answer these questions you should start tracking how often you interrelate with others and take note of the emotional climate as you interact with them. Is it a pleasant exchange, is it rushed, are you smiling, angry, etc.?

Do this for a week or two and then lay it out graphically to see how you work and connect with your team and key stakeholders. There is new research that shows effective teams are based on the patterns and frequency of communication between one another. It is not even about what is being said; it's more about how often and how it occurs. Researchers at MIT are literally able to measure these patterns and variables like tone, posture, emotional resonance to determine if a team is highly effective.

There is another layer to this little experiment based on older research. Focusing on inclusion and exclusion into the in-group provides you awareness of who is being left out and not heard. It should tune you into those unable to contribute because their voice is not being heard. Or conversely, you may find that they have the opportunity to contribute but are unwilling to contribute. Your question then becomes why? Is it because they lack the confidence to do so, or is it because they lack the ability? Answers from this investigation can lead you to strengthening your team and core skills to make you a more effective leader.

Employee Engagement 101

How about this novel approach to engaging your people... try being more personable. Yes, that's it. Try it today. It won't cost you anything just a little time. But it's time well spent. When you walk into your workplace, try actually talking to your people. If it's been a while since you've done it, here's how it might look:

"Good Morning! How are you today?"

Simple. Easy. Breezy. But, here's the hard part; do it while you are looking at them eye to eye. And then wait for a response. Literally, wait the three seconds it takes to get a response. And while you're waiting, be ready listen to what they say. You can build tomorrow's conversation off what you heard today. If your team is virtual; then start your conversation on the phone with, "Hello! How are you today?" (Did you expect something else?) And don't rush to fill the silence. Wait for them. I do it all the time when I call people on the phone, especially customer service reps. Try it; it's amazing to hear how many people never even answer the question. Hold your breath after you ask it and wait.

Most of the time people feel it's just a courtesy that's better to rush through and be done with, but it's certainly not. It is about being real and creating a connection with another person. As leaders, we set the tone for our people. If our people see us as too busy to engage or too frantic to take a moment with them, why should they be inspired by us? By our actions and inattentiveness we show them where they stand in level of importance. I'm not saying that the cafeteria worker should command the same time and attention as your Chairman of the Board, but you should also never demean or devalue anyone by your words or actions. This is leadership at the most basic level.

If you want to build a culture that your people can thrive in, it has to start with mastering the basics. As your leadership culture matures, we can talk more about things like autonomy and purpose. But until then, keep it simple by starting with the easy stuff. If you want to be the leader that positively impacts your people, engage them. Be nice, be human and be real. You'll be amazed at the difference it makes.

Brand Your Learning

What's the learning brand strategy at your place? Do you even have one? Would your employees recognize any of your offerings? Do you differentiate between high-potential development and 'mass development?' Do people want in, or are they forced in?

I continually see organizations that have not done much in the way of branding and marketing their internal programs. They've let them be. And it shows. I still see poorly prepared presentation materials with clip art plastered all over it. It makes me laugh, not the gut-roaring guttural kind, but the sarcastic I can't believe this is serious kind.

Learning and development may be an investment of the corporate dollar, but if we are to believe that it's the people that make the difference in our organizations, then we need to put some money where our mouth is. Developing programs that people want to be a part of makes sense and putting dollars into that development also makes sense. So why is it that we still have courses that look like they were created at the dawn of the internet age?

Why don't we brand our learning so that substance matches style? Do your people even know what you offer? Are they compelled to go to training because of the quality of the content or are they mandated to attend to meet some goal for the year? Could they tell you what it means to be in your high-potential development programs? Do they understand the value that these programs create? If you can't answer yes to these questions, then you need to consider what you're doing to brand and market your professional learning and development offerings.

If the value proposition isn't clear and people can't explain the purpose, then it's time you get clear in the value that you bring and the purpose you serve. And, please, stop showing us the 'butts-in-seat' data. I don't care about how many people attended a course; I care about what they're doing as a result of attending the course. Get to the deeper meaning and you'll get to a clearer purpose.

Where the Real Work Gets Done

The next time you're sitting around thinking about the state of your organization, you should get away from your office and head out to the trenches. What do I mean by the trenches? I mean the shop floor where employees are making products, out in the field where employees are providing customer service calls, or in the call center where employees actually talk to customers to provide support and solve their problems.

Get out to that part of your organization where, as seen by the customer, your company actually DOES what it is in business to do. It's where the work gets done, and it's where all of the strategy thought up in board rooms, conference room and staff meetings actually comes into play. As a leader, it's where you will learn the most about your company, your people and your customers. It's all there for you if you take the time to look and listen.

I just returned from a client plant site where I had an opportunity to speak with some frontline employees over the course of two days. Every time I do this, I am always amazed with the level of complexity they deal with day in and day out. I consistently hear them talking about change and the constant pressures of hitting their metrics, satisfying customers and keeping employees motivated and engaged—day in and day out through all of the changes. The challenge I have always found with the frontline vs. corporate division relationship is the decisions made from corporate tend to feel removed from the realities of how the strategy plays out in the trenches.

I have been on both sides of the fence, and appreciate the challenges that both face. The dynamics that play out on the frontline make implementing any change a difficult proposition. The noise in the system is real, it's intense and can distract employees from the goals they're trying to achieve. It is difficult to sustain focus on any one initiative when you know that it is likely to change in the course of a few weeks or even days. It is doubly difficult to do so when the incentives in place do not align to the effort underway. Yet, somehow, work continues to get done, because the employees have learned systems of interaction and patterns of communication that allow them to effectively manage (or tolerate) all of the change.

Working on the frontline, is not for the feeble-hearted. It takes real guts and requires a resilient mindset. You have to be able to bounce back; you have to be able to deal with the competing pressures from your leadership, your fellow employees and most importantly your customers. Real-work happens in the trenches. A company is only as good as their frontline. Leaders at all levels need to keep this top of mind, and learn new ways to support employees putting direct hands on the products and services and that deal directly with customers.

So take that first step. Get up from your swivel chair, come from behind that computer screen, step out of your office, and spend a day out where the real work gets done.

Setting the Tone

New school coach, old-school hard-noser. Did Greg Schiano, coach of the Tampa Bay Buccaneers pull a bush league stunt out of frustration against the New York Giants, in a game during the 2012 season, or did he set a tone for his club and his players? Did he break unwritten rules of the NFL or did he inspire his team and challenge them to play hard until the last second?

Here's the scenario if you're not much into football. One second left in the game, the Giants are up 41-34 after coming from behind in a big way. Eli Manning goes to kneel to run out the clock and is tripped up by a Bucs defensive lineman who submarines the play in an attempt to knock the ball loose. The unwritten rule in the NFL is that when players are going to take a knee (signaled by the formation they take... usually with only seconds left on the game clock) with the game conceivably out of reach, the other team backs down and lets them. The Giants were incensed when Eli was knocked down on a play where no one really plays, but Schiano insisted that his team play until the final whistle.

So I ask you, is this the case of a new leader who doesn't understand the etiquette of his new 'office,' or is it the case of a new leader trying to establish himself and his team as 'fighters?'

I've gone both ways on this one.

I respect that he's trying to establish himself, but I take issue with the fact that he went against etiquette. Normally, I'm okay with that, I've done it myself from time to time (when it was called for, in my own determination) but in this situation someone could've been pretty seriously hurt. The tipping point for me in deciding against the call was when I heard the sound bites from his players. Most sounded embarrassed and weren't defending the play, but rather took a 'no comment' approach saying, "Coach told us to do it."

It made me wonder about leadership, setting the tone and gaining commitment from your people. My real question isn't whether you agree or not with the call, but instead, how do you think this affects the team, and was it true leadership?

A Label or Ringing Endorsement?

What does it mean to be a high-potential employee in your organization? A hi-po? How does your company define the term? Formally, you may define it as an employee who is ready to take on a role that is significantly more complex than his/her current role.

That is a lot of words, and for most people it does not mean anything. It's simply a grouping together of stuffy, pompous HR words... the strange jargon we like to use. It's lost on most people when we give them the hi-po label but we never tell the hi-po what it means now that they have been given this label. We undermine ourselves by not taking follow on action. We tell you that you are a hi-po, you have lots of runway or headspace and then when the first opportunity comes up to promote you; we put you through the grind.

It is time to simplify our language. To connect it back to the business. If you want to talk about what a high-potential is, start talking about risk. For me, the true definition of high-potential is that you're willing to take a risk on an individual. It means you are willing to put them into a position that may be a stretch. It means you are going to take a chance on them. It does not mean you are going to watch them drown and not give support. But it does mean you are willing to challenge them and see what they've really got.

Think Steve Burke big. At a fairly young age, Disney sent him to France to resurrect Euro-Disney. They gave him a chance. And it paid off; he fixed it by adding wine (you can thank him for that the next time you go to any Disney park) and making other structural changes. There was big money on the line. But he showed promise, and they took the risk on him.

If you believe in your high-potentials, show them. Challenge them and push them. You will be impressed with the level of effort you'll get as a result. People are motivated by challenges, especially your hi-pos. They want to do more; they can take on that more complex role. So hook it up and give them a chance. Take the uncertain risk on your top talent now... to gain the high reward of their loyalty and retention in return later. You will not be let down.

On Being High-Potential

Only a third of the companies in the US actually let you know that you're high-potential. And of those companies that do publicly covet their high-potentials, most don't really give you the details of what being a high-potential means. Being named a high-potential is good... but only great if there is a definition and a set of expectations that accompany that designation.

The fact this matters deeply in the workplace shouldn't even be a debate at this point. Not being transparent about where people stand in your organization is making matters worse. If you're not telling them what their future growth potential is in the organization, you leave them to fill in the blanks. And if you leave that up to them, they will most likely think one of two extremes:

"I'm a superstar", or "I'm not a part of the organization's future plan". And trust me, they are watching and listening to everything you do as their leader. Walking the talk has never been more of an imperative for leaders in today's workplace and workforce.

If Gen X employees sense that they're not one of the superstars, or if they somehow see other people being treated differently, they will certainly want to know why. Sure, you can choose not to tell them. But be prepared for the sentiment of "you don't want to tell me, that's cool, I'm going to start looking elsewhere" to work through your team or organization (remember about the informal network). And, those few intrepid souls will take control of their career in view of others who just needed visual motivation to do just the same. And with that, the exodus has begun.

So explain to me the risk reward here. You can keep it a secret and your people will talk about it. That's when the rumor mill swirls. Two cultures develop; the one you think you have and the one that your people will develop on their own.

Alternatively, you can open the doors, be transparent about your process and actually tell your people how the process works. Sure, some may not be happy with what they hear, but at least it's the truth. And isn't that what we should be telling people? Well, we all know the answer to that question.

A Bus Token and a Title

I remember hearing very early in my life that "a token and a title will only get you a ride on the bus… if you don't forget the token". I never really thought much about what it meant when I first heard it, but I came to understand fully later in my career that it's not the title that counts.

It's the work that you do, it's who you are and it's where you want to go that really matters. It's one of the reasons that as I was building my career, I never turned down an opportunity to talk about an open role with a recruiter. I learned to become "title agnostic" in a way. You want to draw high-potentials to your organization, get over the grandiose titles, move beyond structural hierarchies, and get with allowing people to board the bus at their own stop.

Organizational hierarchies worked during the post-WWII era. In the age of globalization, they're not so relevant. In an age of diffused networks and ever-faster flows of information, you can't stop people from interacting with one another because of a title. Gen X and Gen Y aren't wowed by your corner office or your fancy title. If you hold so rigidly to your organizational structure that you won't let 'junior' staff converse with senior leaders, we're walking right out the door.

We want to know what you've done to set you apart from others. We're more impressed with how you align your work and your values than with the title on your business card. We want to know how you've made an impact on this world and on others. You may revere a senior executive, but do it because of who they are, not what title they go by in the organization. They put their pants on just like the rest of us. They make mistakes just like the rest of us.

If you're looking to attract high-potential talent to your organization, don't try to woo or impress them with titles and offices. Get them to come because the work you have is meaningful and challenging. You'll keep them there much longer that way. Once they get there, let them live a little. Don't try and control how they navigate the organization. You may be surprised what they bring to the table. Give them a token, and just let them ride the bus.

What Leadership Does to Those You Lead (Setting the Tenor)

You Hired Me... Now Stop Trying to Change Me

You just hired me, so why are you trying to change me? I'm assuming you brought me in because you knew I could do the job, so why is it that you're trying so hard to make me conform? Why is it that you're doing your best to make me be someone I'm not? If I had known this, I would NOT have accepted this job.

Your employees shouldn't be thinking these thoughts. It's not healthy and it's counterproductive. But this is the dilemma we face in our professional lives. At some point, we have to make the tough choice. Can we hold on to who we are and still lead a successful and meaningful life? Or do we need to conform to our organization's culture, or to the wishes of a boss? Do we need to be constantly "on," do we need to "show up well" in every meeting and in every situation?

There comes a time in your professional career when the eyes are upon you and you have to make a legitimate decision about where you want to go. Do you want to "conform" and give up part of yourself to be viewed as a player? Or are you more interested in staying true to yourself and potentially being viewed as disengaged, a bad hire, or not competent?

These are conversations that happen every year in corporate America. There's the internal struggle that plays out, and then there's the conversations that take place behind closed doors. This is where people start questioning your commitment. It's where decisions get made based on how well you "acclimate" to the corporate culture.

You were hired because you're smart and qualified, but if you want to stick around you may need to learn how to play the game. For many of us, this is where things go wrong. We don't fully commit to one way or the other. We refuse to fully conform, but we're not ready or we are afraid to try something new. The simple decision is do I change how I work, or do I change where and with whom I work?

Make a decision on what you are going to do and don't let it linger. If you do, the longer you wait... the worse it will become.

Now, We Really Value You

I watched as a friend went through an interesting lesson. I had been coaching him about his career and talking to him about what was next for him. Over the course of the past month, he had been courted by a start-up company that was growing rapidly. The company was seen as highly creative, innovative but very young. There was stability in the organization, it had a very mature parent company; but there was autonomy. The role was interesting and was going to provide great cross-functional opportunities and there was talk about rotating through different roles in the organization.

Sounded like a no brainer to me when we discussed the role and talked about where he is in his current organization. But something unexpected happened when he went to leave his company. They countered and they countered strong. Quite honestly, he was surprised. I think he was hoping they would, but I don't think he expected what happened. He was forced into a decision that he didn't expect he would have to make. It's at that moment, he realized that he had a future with his current employer.

He had done well with them, but always had some trouble reading the tea leaves and getting a sense of what his future held there. So when the new company came calling, he was open to listen, and then they pitched him, and got him to a point where he could see himself there. I know he analyzed all angles, reflected thoughtfully on both options and ultimately made the decision that was best for his family; that didn't make it an easy decision. But ultimately, he realized it was the right decision.

I hear these stories all the time, and it always astounds me that your value is not fully recognized until you are about to walk. Never forget that you must own your personal career succession plan. If you want to avoid being stuck where you don't want to be, consider how you can play a good offense in your organization in order to make things happen and get yourself unstuck.

Waiting and hoping will not bring you the career that you want... you must actively seek and find your career success with passion.

What Leadership Does to Your Head (The Shadows of Poor Leadership)

The Proclivity to Foster Fence Sitting

Nobody wants to be told they are average. It has become a negative connotation in our vernacular, and deservedly so in some ways. But when we start force ranking people we put 70% of our employees into that space. We tell them they are average. We give them a standard 3% raise and then pay them no attention. Because we just assume that they will keep chugging away, running the engine and making things happen. That's the easiest path... no resistance and often in a leadership lull we let it happen by default.

In most places, those in the 70% go unnoticed. They become your grinders, but they are not your superstars. But for those sitting on the fence, all they need is a little love. So find a way to give it to them. It's typical in our society to focus on the highs and the lows; we tend to ignore the middle. It's tough to get people to pay attention to you. If you are someone in a position to do something about the 70% it's time to start working on it.

This group may not be your bench strength right now, but they straddle the fence between being ready for more and for becoming disengaged. Organizations have a responsibility to work with this group to make sure that they're headed in the right direction. If you can bring part of this group up, not letting them remain on the fence, and get them the experiences and skills that are important to your organization, you can start to move the needle in positive direction to address your talent shortage.

This type of work takes time and obviously scale. You can't do everything for everyone. But, you can and you should start to offer targeted solutions to the fence sitters.

It does not have to be done on a grand scale, but it all needs to be well thought out and consistent. If you can get these valuable employees off the fence, then you can get them engaged. All it takes is just some time, attention, and coaxing.

Did You See Your Shadow?

Change sometimes comes early here in the Northeast. The winter season might be harsh, or even brutal. And talking about it only increases the likelihood that something strange is a brewing. We do our best to be ready for either event; the warmth of spring, or an extended winter.

When all signs are pointing to an early spring the change is the easy one. It stays light longer; the temperatures gets warmer and people tend to have an added spring in their step. Change isn't always easy. But it's always imminent. So my question is how well does your organization embrace change and are you ready for the hard change?

We can all talk a good game, but in reality very few of us manage change well. The fact is the majority of our change initiatives fail miserably. We don't communicate them well enough, leaders don't fully buy in, it becomes the flavor of the month and it quickly dies on the vine as soon as the weather dips back to freezing.

In this hyper competitive environment it feels like we are moving so fast that we don't give ourselves the proper time to reflect, plan and prepare for what's ahead. In most companies I work with, it's all about pace. March ahead, get it done and if it isn't the right solution we'll reset. This may work in the high tech world where new products are developed almost by the minute. But in most other industries you don't have the culture to support this. And your culture is critical to supporting any type of change. You probably already know it before you even step into the change; whether the initiative will spring to life or be sucked up into the jaws of your culture.

Take a few extra moments; reflect, plan and prepare for what's next and then make sure you get out and sell it. But remember that selling it isn't enough. You need to support it. You're not Punxsutawney Phil, you can't be afraid of the shadow you cast. Embrace the change.

Call it Star Power

In research published in the Journal of Leadership and Organizational Development, three researchers from George Washington University challenge the age-old assumption that people leave jobs because of their direct boss. What they found is that people are more inclined to leave because of a more senior functional leader in their organization.

If the research is in fact true and holds up to what are sure to be challenges from other academics, this has some profound implications for the way we recruit, develop and retain leaders at all levels in our organization.

First and foremost, our senior leaders need to be made explicitly aware of the shadow that they cast. They are under the microscope more than they ever realized and their actions, or lack thereof, have a huge ripple effect on the climate of an organization.

Secondly, we need to ensure that we have the right leaders in those roles. They need to be stars; "A" players. Because "A" players attract other "A" players. We all want to work for someone great, someone who intuitively gets it and challenges us to be at our best. The more credibility the leader has in their field, the better. This means that we need to help our leaders build credibility, help them establish themselves both internally and externally.

Stars have magnetism about them. They draw others to them; it is a gravitational force that helps keep people engaged and willing to drive themselves harder. When that star fades, it loses its pull and people will no longer follow. But we can help keep our stars shining bright with a few easy tactics:

1. Be on the ground with the employees, help the leadership team know what people are feeling, seeing, hearing
2. Remove any noise in the system that gets in the way of people doing their work
3. Remind leaders of their downstream impact

Keep these things in mind, and you will continue to bring out the best in your leaders and their people. If you are in the market for a new leader, remember that you want someone who has that magnetic draw about them.

Star Power is not easy to describe, but you will know it... if and when you see it.

* * *

There are many folks put in positions of leadership and they are not leaders. It happens all the time, when people are promoted based on their seniority. They've been here long enough, or you've been with the team long enough and there is an opening, and we'll reward you for your years of service and dedication as an individual contributor or some type of specialist. We are going to reward you now by giving you a team of people to manage. I think that's one of the worst things that can happen to someone who is not prepared to be a leader: when someone is a really good individual contributor, you promote them into a leadership role and you expect them to do equally well, without giving them the tools with which to be successful. Namely interpersonal skills and the things we're talking about in this book.

Something that I heard in boot camp many moons ago rings true. In the absence of leadership, you must lead. That has stuck in my mind over the decades. You're going to get into positions where someone needs to do something and there's a pause because the current leader is inept and does not know what to do or is oblivious that action is needed... so a true leader has to step forward. If there is a person who is entitled or in position or even in caricature who is supposed to be the leader, and that person shirks their responsibility or backs away from the table or walks away, you should not be content to see that happen. If you are a person who aspires to be a leader and not a follower, you should instead say, "If you're not to be the leader, then allow me to do it."

A long time ago, somebody told me, "The world steps aside for anyone who seemingly has a plan." If nothing else, to see what they're going to do. Just out of morbid curiosity. As adults and as adult leaders, and quite frankly, as a culture, we all want to follow someone who seems to know what they're doing. It's an intoxicating thing for many of us to be led by an effective leader. I can't stand it, personally, when I see someone who drops the ball, who is afraid to lead, who is afraid to make the hard choice, afraid to make any choice. I have stepped into that space and oftentimes, and sometimes I've gotten my hand slapped (I'll keep it G-rated) for stepping up, stepping in.

I also think that every great leader in history steps forward to do something because they believe that what they were doing was right. Whether the outcomes, the means, the construct was legal, moral, or ethical, set that aside, each leader—even the most notorious of such—all did what they did because they believed they were needed. They believed they were trying to change things for the better (even if their plan was for them to gain the most of the 'better'). It's amazing to see that and think about when somebody gets put in a position to be a leader, and they have not seen this, thought this, felt this, and they become paralyzed unto themselves and not do anything. I can't sit idly by and watch that, so I often throw myself into the mix. Much like writing my first book. I felt like someone should be the voice for Gen-X with regard to talent management or that intersection where generational diversity and career and personal development intersect. There was an absence of leadership in that aspect, and I led. Hopefully, if you ever face a situation where the leader is absent or just won't serve... you'll be prepared to step up.

* * *

It sticks with me. People have heard it all the time. I can't remember who it's attributed to. It's one of those Peter Drucker management-guru types (no disrespect intended towards Peter Drucker). "You lead people but you manage projects." I think no truer words have been spoken about the difference between management and leadership. In the world of work the title Project Manager is well-known and understood but you never hear so much that someone is a "People Manager." If they do, it's almost like calling the HR department "personnel." It's an anachronism in my mind. But when I think about the difference between leading people and managing projects, it's simple. With a project, you're directing and you're driving towards results. You're trying to get something done. Get the right thing done, if you will. Whereas leading people is more about inspiration. You're trying to help people do things right. There is a difference there. You lead people because you're bringing them along. You are inspiring. You are mentoring. You're coaching. You're helping them do things the right way. Excuse me, do the right things the right way. As opposed to managing projects, where it's very much about the brain. Leading is about the heart. You're leading with the heart. Leadership is more warmth and the human spirit. Management is more about checking the box.

Here's something I experienced that was very startling. It happened not so very long ago at a very large organization I had the opportunity to be a part of for a while. I was in a large meeting with a bunch of other executives and the senior executive of the function, let's say, within this organization, stood up and said. "I'm really happy to be here at this leadership program saying a few words." That's good, I thought. But what he said next was shocking to me. "I love being at the leadership program, but overall, we need more managers at this organization. We don't need more leaders." As I think about that, it still shocks me.

To say that shows this is someone who is just wired completely differently. Here is someone who stands up and says, "Listen, we don't need any more leaders. What we need are managers." I was hanging on the edge of my chair, waiting for this guy to give some qualification to what he said. His thinking, his bend on this, is everyone who is a leader wants to inspire and to influence, but no one is in a position to try to get the work done. I thought that was interesting, where he was saying we need more managers. It's almost like I wanted to drop the word "micro" into it.

We need more micro-managers, because I think that, if you do leadership the right way, and you really inspire and influence people, you'll have the most power in the world to actually help people get things done, because you've inspired them to excellence. You've influenced them to accomplishment, to achievement. And if you can do it that way, you can really move forward. Not get mired down in the trivia of micro-management.

Unfortunately, what happens for many folks is they think managing and leading are the same thing. In reality, they're not. One is very much about heart. One is very much about head, or mind. It's unfortunate that some can't make the leap. I think it's indicative of what happens when you take someone who is an individual contributor, who has the skills to be a manager—to work behind the scenes with data and spreadsheets and inanimate objects, if you will, to get things done, you know, your classic project manager—and you turn them into a leader of people, it doesn't go so very well. The reason it doesn't go so very well is because that person is ill-equipped to do the job. You can't take someone who has never flown a plane before, who has spent their entire life watching planes through the sky, and then put them behind the controls of a plane of any size and expect them to be successful, just because they've seen it done before. I think that's what happens, and the risk any organization exposes itself to, when they take someone who is a really good manager of things and make them a leader of people.

KEYS TO UNLOCK THE DOOR TO EFFECTIVE LEADERSHIP

17) Do What You Say --- Words must be more than just wind. You can talk. But then you must "do". If you don't do that and do it consistently... then you will get the respect that you deserve, which is none. Companies can operate with leaders that aren't respected—but it's doubtful the organization will thrive under that type of leadership (or lack thereof). Be the type of leader that backs up their words with action. Better yet, lead by example... show your people you know what you're talking about and care about what happens to them and the company and less about how you sound. And you know what... your clients, customers and the market are watching, too, and will also respond in some way based on your actions (not your words).

18) View Your Team Members as People First --- The flip side of action is engagement with the people you lead that support the action. There has to be engagement and meaningful interaction across all levels—the right balance of both leads to a more effective team and organization, which will reflect, ultimately, on the performance of the leaders.

19) Encourage and Celebrate Leaderful Moments --- Become the type of leader that places more importance on the individual performance and less on their title. Most importantly—treat yourself the same way. Don't get puffed up because of your title or position; instead show everyone that you earned respect by who you are and what you do as opposed to what's on your business card.

20) Share Your Leadership Journey as a Path for Others --- If you follow the advice given in these keys—you will have done much to become a better person and more effective leader. What's more you will develop the type of star power that draws good people to you. You will have the most loyal colleagues and people to work for you. And remember it's the team that you surround yourself with that wins the game for you and your organization. Value them as much or more than you value your contribution.

CONCLUSION

Without Character & Integrity... Who Are We?

"Only those who dare to fail greatly can ever achieve greatly."

—Robert F. Kennedy

Mirror, Mirror

Are we the Man in the mirror that we can face each day with direct eye contact? Or are we like the Wizard of Oz in the 1939 movie... the Man behind the curtain... *"Pay no attention to that man behind the curtain..."* a weak man behind a façade.

In the mirror, over time, we see the change in us. Change is the only constant in life—few things are static. But one thing must be. Who you are inside and what you choose to be perceived as by others.

Integrity Matters in Leadership

As a democracy, who we choose to lead us is very important (I don't think it's possible to overstate that). During the course of the 2012 presidential campaign I became a big supporter of Politifact (and you thought I was going to say a candidate). I checked the site regularly; because I felt (and still feel) like half of what is said by both parties is either a blatant lie or it's a twisted accusation of the other's account. I don't like it, but it's what American politics is. It's not what American politics has become, it's always been this way in some form or another, but now we're so inundated with information that it's hard not to notice it. And it's a real shame. When I think about leadership, the first value that comes to my mind is integrity. It matters, and

129

most importantly it matters when you are in a position responsible for serving others... for being their leader.

Unfortunately, we've created a system bent on sound bites and quick hitting verbal assaults. We like the one-liner and a good zinger, but as leaders, this isn't realistic. It doesn't provide context and it doesn't enable people to understand the whole story, the full account of what's happened or of what's been said. The details are critical elements to any story (and this is coming from someone who prefers the big picture view) we need to be able to speak truth in our politics, our boardrooms and our offices. We need people to stand up for integrity. Without it, there's no trust, and without trust there's no real communication.

Beyond the political realm, take a look at what's happened in the Citi Boardroom in 2012 with Vikram Pandit. A day after announcing corporate earnings, the CEO abruptly resigns. Millions of dollars of investment decisions were just made the day before based on the implied trust that Pandit would continue to lead the company and build for a better future. It didn't happen. He bailed. But why? Early indications are a lack of trust from within the boardroom. They had seen enough of Pandit, which is their prerogative, but it brings to question their integrity when both parties knowingly go into the earnings call and act as if nothing is happening. Investors depend on reliable and accurate information to make decisions, and this has impact on too many people.

Leaders need to step up and act with integrity when so much is on the line politically or financially, because integrity matters.

The Legacy We Leave Behind

Are the tracks you leave revered or do they rush to sweep them away.

Let's go back to that mirror. Have you looked in it lately and really asked yourself, "Who am I?" Did you like your answer? Is it consistent with your efforts to become who you want to be? Does it match up to how others would answer that same question about you? What is said is indeed your professional brand. And like it or not, you are primarily defined by the workplace perception of others. No doubt you can influence that perception, but it's much more common each day to take a hit to your brand than it is to gain favor or build your brand.

And each hit can last for a long time. Each ding gets stuck in people's minds and it comes out of their mouths. It's not often you hear about the good things people do, but people are quick to point out flaws or things done wrong. So, if you're stuck or in the crosshairs, it's time to actively manage your brand, influence those perceptions and get people thinking less about who you are and more about who you want to be—who you can be, for them and for yourself. Rebuilding or repairing your professional brand is not for the thin-skinned... but it can be done.

Like any home improvement project it starts with you and a look around your current place—your situation. You have to be able to answer the question honestly of who you are and if you don't like your answer, you need to do some deep reflection and from that create a blueprint. Figure out who you want to be and start making small, conscientious and continuous changes to your new brand daily. "Mind the Gap" between the You of today (version 1.0) and the You of the near future (version 2.0) because there may be a large void there that until now has gone unnoticed by you (though chances are others can point it out). At the end of the day, you have to manage those perceptions before you get anyone else invested in your career aspirations.

Start poking around and learn what the "word on the street" is about you.

How do you show up to other people? Ask colleagues close to you and knowledgeable of your brand to share how they would define what they see, feel, or hear about your brand. Then decide if those words are acceptable to you as a definition. If so, that's great! If not... now is the time to put your brand under construction. Start working on it by hand; actively and consistently working on who you want to become. Your next career move may very well start by taking a good look in the mirror, and taking a few figurative trips to your favorite home (self) improvement store.

Will You Leave A Legacy?

In every profession, there is a transcendent superstar. Someone who leaves a legacy behind, someone who alters the course of the profession and inspires future generations. With the Olympics, it is easy to start talking about transcendent star power with the likes of Michael Phelps, Usain Bolt, Lebron James, Misti May-Treanor and Kerri Walsh Jennings grabbing our attention. Watching Phelps swim his last race this past Olympics got me thinking about the impact that I hope to leave on my profession.

I listened to Phelps in an interview talking about why he was done this time around; why he was retiring at the relatively young age of 27. He said that he had accomplished all he set out to accomplish and he was not up for staring at a black line under water for four hours a day anymore. I can fully appreciate that sentiment and realization. The commitment to excel like that takes hours upon hours of commitment and dedication. In the corporate world, it is difficult to sustain that edge. Most of us are not in a position by age 27 to have claimed legacy status.

So how do we maintain the commitment, drive and energy needed to sustain ourselves over the long term? It is a difficult task, and there is no easy solution. But part of the solution rests in our ability to slow down, recharge and refocus. It takes time and effort to learn how to slow ourselves down in order to maintain a hyper competitive speed when we are ready to get back at it. I like to compare it to the maturation of an NFL quarterback. You hear all the time how the game "slows" down for the greats. It gets easier, because they learn how to process everything they see, filter what is not important and take action when the time is ready. They do this all, by the way, in a matter of seconds. The point is; it takes time and practice to get yourself to this point.

If you want to make an impact and leave a lasting legacy behind, you need to learn what drives you and what motivates you. It's also imperative that you learn how to recharge and refresh. It's a practice you should invest in every day. The effort you put in now will pay off longer term as you build your legacy.

How to Work With Gen Y

It's becoming increasingly important for us to be able to work across generations in the workplace. The Boomers are starting to leave, but there not all gone, Gen X is ready to assume more of the leadership roles, and Gen Y is getting antsy. The stagnant labor market hasn't made this situation any easier. It has an adverse impact on internal job movement as well, further complicating the cross-generational relationships. We have to assume that in the next few years we'll see a turn in the labor market.

The thing about the impatient Gen Yers is that you must give them the rope to hang themselves, but be close enough to catch them. You have to be willing to empower them, and you have to let them learn from experience. The more opportunities that you give them to learn, the more you'll see them hustle. Gen Y wants to make an impact.

According to one high performing young professional that I mentor, and a member of Gen Y, "there's a misconception about my generation. People think we've been spoon fed our entire lives. People make generalizations about us, and unfortunately they stick. The end result is our leaders are scared to give us the rope to get our work done. They don't empower us. The irony is all we want is to be empowered and to show we can do it. If we want to make generalizations, we should talk about the hyper competitive environments that many of us grew up in. Yes, we may have been praised more than most, but we also learned pretty quickly what it was like to deal with peer pressure and competitive situations within our peer group."

Give your people the rope to get their work done, challenge them and give them opportunities to shine, but you need to let them fail too. They'll learn from it, be better off for it, and you'll have shown you have faith in their abilities. Gen Y doesn't need praise, they need faith, they want to know that you trust in them and you believe in them. Show them and be there for them when things don't work.

As Gen X leaders we must make their work meaningful and we have to challenge them. Don't just dish out the rote work. Challenge Gen Y. They want to feel involved in what's important.

Many Gen Yers probably believe they're ready to lead, but coach them and talk to them about getting time under their belt and the experiences necessary to lead effectively. Paint them the picture of why it's important to have lived experiences in the trenches. Let them know it's like muscle memory, the more you experience, the more you can draw on. Most importantly make sure the experiences you expose them to have meaning. Expose them to leadership; bring them along to the important meetings. Help them see the big picture. Give them insight into career development. Talk to them about the importance of building a portfolio of broad experiences before worrying about leadership. It's easier to build those experiences early in your career and it will pay off five-fold later in life.

Getting To Where You Want To Be (As a Leader)

It's so easy to get wrapped up in our day-to-day, that we rarely take the time to reflect on where we are, how we got here and where we're headed. What kind of goals have you really targeted for the year? And by goals, I'm talking both personally and professionally.

If you have set some goals, how are you moving toward them? Have you started to take action yet? Have you thought about the specifics of getting them done? How much time have you put into analyzing your environment? On a professional level, what's next for you? Where do you want to take your career? How have you defined success? Are you living up to the goals you set for yourself and most importantly, are you staying true to you? Are you grateful, happy, content, unhappy or miserable? Or are you stuck in the middle? I know... a lot of questions but all worthy of thinking about and answering honestly.

If you haven't taken more than a fleeting moment to think about your goals, try setting aside two hours of your time, at some point in your week, to really reflect on where you are. It's a life changing experience. You may be successful, but at what cost? Are you happy, are those around you happy? Use the time to think about where you want to go professionally. Start thinking three to five years out and plan backwards. What steps can you take today to set the foundation for tomorrow? Think about the people that you can reach out to for help; you're not in this alone. Moving forward isn't a solo event, it requires that you network and plan appropriately.

My goal with what I'm telling you is to help you reflect, ask you the tough questions and challenge you to make the decisions that will make you happiest. If you're an employer reading this, my goal is to help you think about how to get the most out of your people by creating the structures and processes needed to cultivate a vibrant, motivated and grateful workforce. It can be done.

Going the Extra Mile to Succeed

Did you go the extra mile this week? If not, what stopped you? Was it a peer, a boss, your family, or was it you? Most likely it was you. We hold ourselves back from doing extraordinary things every day. But why? What stops us from going the extra mile? What stops us from doing something bigger or better?

I would venture that 90% of the time, it's our own self-imposed limitations.

We stop ourselves from exceeding expectations, and then we look for excuses about why. It's natural, we all do it, and what is worse is we do it every day. It's easy to blame others. We look at situations and easily jump into excuse mode. It did not work out because of so and so or such and such. But that's BS, and we know it.

I have been fortunate to not get caught in this pattern. As a consultant, my expertise is getting to solutions, working around obstacles, and creating circumstances that are favorable so that everyone wins. As an entrepreneur, I go the extra mile day in and day out. But I'm smart about it. My time and energy are finite. I know not to stretch myself too thin. I have learned to focus on what is most important in the moment. My mentors keep me honest in this respect.

By relentless networking, I am always hunting for additional blue chippers to add to my network. I seek out people that are going to push me in the right direction. I am referring to people who are not happy with minimal effort, who do not wait around for career success to find them. I surround myself with go-getters, entrepreneurs, contrarians, and rainmakers... those people who have a burning desire to bust up bureaucracy. I connect best with these intrepid souls who refuse to be victims of self. This is how I have personally avoided getting stuck in the middle and how I now, as an executive coach, can lead others out of their own valley of despair.

By setting realistic short-term career goals, you can achieve or reassess success often. You look at the people in my network and with whom you most often interact. You should want to be with the people who are willing to push you that extra mile when it matters most. You want to have those people in your professional network who are willing to push back their own limitations because they want to see just how far they can go.

If you are really ready to push past your limitation, then it's time to cut the dead weight from your network, remove the albatross from around the neck of your career passion, and build yourself a high performing support team. If you do that, you will be on the right path to being able to look in the mirror, and not make excuses for failing to go the distance.

Setting Marathon Goals for Your Team

I have a friend. He runs. In fact, he runs marathons. We got to talking about his training and reasons he likes marathons and I have not been able to wrap my head around the 'why' for so long. I never really understood the appeal.

But, I was interested in hearing him tell me about the commitment and dedication it takes to run long distances. It is more about mental strength than physical ability after a certain distance. His take was that if you can run ten miles, you can run 26.2, the only thing holding you back is you.

I looked skeptically at him. I'm not a runner, but the thought sounded a bit crazy. That is when he made the connection to what I do. He told me he breaks down every run, whether it is a race, or a training run, into small chunks. It's the only way to make it through. He plays tricks on his mind, and he sets small goals for himself. Just as he is about to reach one goal, he crafts a new one further ahead. He looks for the next tree a few hundred yards away, or looks for a bend in the terrain.

Through this, he does a few things that, as an organizational development professional, really interest me:

1. He sets a macro goal to accomplish (race day)

2. He creates a very specific, yet achievable training plan with mileposts to guide him
3. He rewards his hard work with off days and recognizes the importance of rest on his body and mind
4. During every run, he sets smaller objectives for himself
5. He is a part of a community that talks to one another about what's working and what's not

After talking with him, I reflected on how we talk about change in an organization and how we are supposed to lay out comprehensive plans. We do not always do this, but we could. We should be setting strategic goals at the macro level. But we should also have a set of micro goals, objectives and tactics that we clearly lay out in front of our employees. More importantly, we should celebrate with them at each marker. We need to make them believe that 26.2 miles is achievable even if they only feel like they are ready for ten miles.

As leaders (or those who wish to become one) you have to touch people in such a way that each day they become incrementally better in some way. That means you must do the leaderly things each and every day... and everyone's watching. If you are worthy, they will follow your lead.

A FINAL THOUGHT
(AND PATRIOTIC WISH)

"Great leaders are almost always great simplifiers, who can cut through argument, debate, and doubt to offer a solution everybody can understand. "

—General Colin Powell

Abraham Lincoln said: *"If I had eight hours to chop down a tree, I'd spend six sharpening my axe"*. Our military veterans who served as NCOs and Officers had to 'sharpen' their leadership skills every day. In the military, errors in judgment or leadership mistakes often have the most extreme consequences. No organization is as unforgiving of poor leadership as the military.

Hiring Excellence... Hiring Our Veterans

So making veteran's and military experience something you seek not only simplifies the process... it also generally will lead to a better "hire". And it's more than nice to see companies starting to ramp up their efforts to hire American veterans. As a 10-year Navy veteran, when I answered the call to defend our freedom some 20 years ago, I answered it willingly. I didn't answer it just for myself; I answered it because I know personally that freedom is not free. I took the oath of enlistment and joined America's Navy because I was stirred to serve something greater than myself. I answered the call to serve during the first Gulf War because there is no greater nation than the United States of America.

Having worn the uniform, I will not, and cannot ever forget the sacrifices that veterans have made to our country. So I write to encourage employers to remember our veterans as they fill their open positions. I know how difficult the transition from military to civilian life can be, and that is why I am proud to see initiatives underway like Hire Heroes (www.hireheroes.org).

To me, this initiative couldn't be more beneficial to both sides. This initiative also could not be timelier as a means to close the talent gap that exists in our current workforce. Veterans get stable employment and the chance to ease their transition back to civilian life, while the companies get true heroes and proven leaders. Who knows leadership better than the US Armed Forces? No one. Not GE, not 3M, not J&J. Veterans bring an increased amount of talent and credibility to your organization.

We veterans come with a deep-seated knowledge in how to get things done and how to lead others. It may take some time to transition from the leadership style of the Armed Forces to that of Corporate America, but that's a transition that can be easily supported through coaching and with time. We also come with a keen sense of what performance under pressure looks like. We know when and how to turn it on, when to get serious and how to get the job done. Most importantly, we know how to read situations, we know when to move quickly with a sense of urgency, or pause for more information.

If you hire a hero, you're getting top of the line talent that is dedicated, driven, and disciplined to making the transition. Sure, you as an employer may need to help support that transition, and you may need to do it in ways that you wouldn't do for other employees, but in the end you're getting top talent that you can count on for their experience, and training to make themselves, and your organization better. When you hire a hero, you get an employee that less likely to be stuck in the middle between what they want, and who they need to be and better able to contribute greatly to your organization.

As a final thought, I want to give a huge shout out to all of our veterans and their families that have sacrificed so much for us. Thank you all and may God continue to bless you. To my readers and followers, if you have not worn the uniform of our nation, I hope you took an opportunity to thank a veteran for all of the contributions and sacrifices our heroes have made to keep our country great.

And to my fellow veterans, I render a hand salute and sound off with a loud "Bravo Zulu" to you for your continued honor, courage, and commitment.

More from Curtis L. Odom, Ed.D.

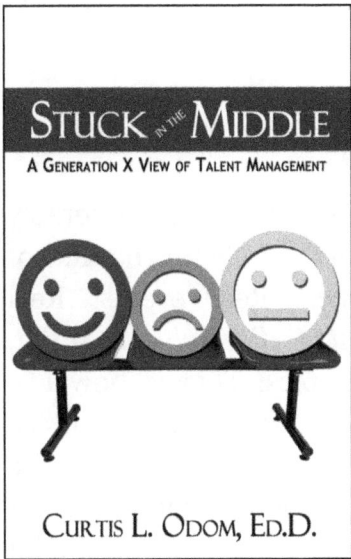

STUCK ᴵᴺ ᵀᴴᴱ **MIDDLE**

A GENERATION X VIEW OF TALENT MANAGEMENT

CURTIS L. ODOM, ED.D.

Part of making things happen as an individual, in your career, or as a company is taking a hard look at things and saying, *"These are my flaws. These are my shortcomings. These are the self-defeating actions where I've shot my success in the foot."* Any person or company who says they've never done those things is hindering their success, ruining their achievement, and unwittingly keeping themselves stuck in the middle.

The unwillingness to do a hard current state assessment is a barrier between getting what you want and continuing to lack what you need. Finding that progress gap is the secret ingredient in the magic formula for understanding what it is that you need (not necessarily what you want) and then taking the steps to get that result (which leads to what you want). Talent management is indeed a business imperative to build and grow a successful organization... but more importantly, it's also a personal imperative for professionals to build successful careers.

When people don't employ personal talent management in the way of owning their own succession plan; when companies and organizations don't build and sustain an integrated talent management strategy; they remain stuck in the middle; somewhere between who they are and who they want to be. How to get unstuck, how to break free from the middle is what individuals and organizations often don't understand. That critical understanding (and ability to take action on it to improve your situation) is what you'll find in this book as told through the eyes of a member of Generation X.

Author's Note:

I think the best way to teach is to provide examples... preferably real and not hypothetical ones constructed purely for the sake of answering a question. Real experience. Real events. Real decisions... with real outcomes. *'What I did, why I did it, and what happened next'* kind of examples. That is how I've approached this book you have in your hands. There will be some, what I feel are astute, Generation X observations on life and certainly on career at it relates to talent management but these are only part of what I want to share with you. I meet a lot of people who, like me, are Gen Xers who are trying to figure out *"How do I make it in corporate America?"*

I have had career success and reached fairly senior positions for *'someone of my age'* with more than one Fortune 100 company. So people come to me and ask, *"What does it take to get to where you are?"* How did I do it? Did I have to sell my soul, strike a deal with the devil, or some different compromising scenario that was traded in an effort for quick success? And then I tell them my career story, which you will find in this book. It is a story steeped in my passion to help organizations solve the dilemma of how and when to buy, build, or borrow the talent they need, while not losing focus on running their business today. This story and the same passion will speak to individuals as well and give them insights and actionable advice on applying proven talent management principles to improve the trajectory of their own careers.

MIND THE GAP

GENERATIONS

GETTING BUSINESS RESULTS IN
MULTIGENERATIONAL ORGANIZATIONS

Curtis L. Odom, Ed.D.

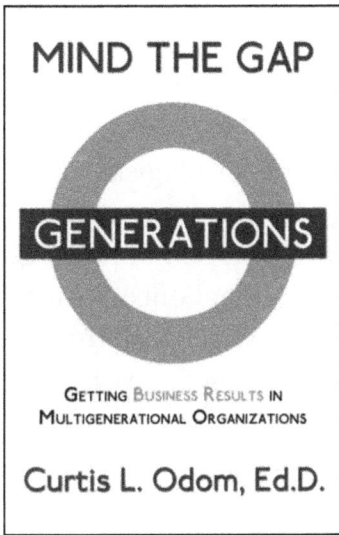

When we talk about the generations that make up our society (and workforce), the myths are just as important as the general truths. These myths are very powerful because they shape how we look at generations. They form in these spaces of misunderstanding between them. We must recognize and acknowledge the gaps that exist. If we focus on the commonalities instead of the differences, we can arrive at a place where all generations can thrive.

What are the challenges with a generationally diverse workforce? What is the gap we're minding? How do we mind this generational gap, use our understanding of it, so we get business results? Many organizations I've worked with, and senior colleagues I've talked to, struggle to work through how to get the best business results from an organization made up of many different generations that want different things. Today, so many organizations are flatter and freer of hierarchy. Employees once segregated by age and position now work more closely together. The flatter the organization, the more it takes to effectively execute a business strategy.

This book addresses simply what organizations and leaders in organizations can do to focus on minding the gap to get the best business results from their multigenerational employees.

About the Author

Dr. Curtis L. Odom is Principal and Managing Partner of the Boston based consultancy, Prescient Strategists, LLC. Curtis has over 15 years of international experience in cultural integration, change management, organizational effectiveness, talent management, and performance consulting as a practitioner, researcher, author, and speaker.

Curtis is an expert change leader with extensive experience leading and implementing large-scale change. Known for his practical expertise, Curtis is a sought after consultant to organizations in change strategy implementation, organization development, leadership/executive development, career coaching, culture change, training and development, and group facilitation.

Curtis has significant depth in strategic and tactical application of cultural integration, change management, organizational effectiveness, talent management, and performance consulting to maximize organizational investments in human capital. Curtis credits his 10 years of military service in the United States Navy for his solid foundation in strategic planning and tactical application of organizational development, change management, and the employ of blended learning frameworks.

Curtis earned a doctorate of education from Pepperdine University, graduating Phi Delta Kappa, and has been industry certified as a Human Capital Strategist (HCS) and Strategic Workforce Planner (SWP) from the Human Capital Institute.

Curtis is also an active member of the Alliance of Mergers and Acquisition Advisors, Association of Change Management Professionals, and American Mensa. As a testament to his professional brand, Curtis was awarded the high distinction of being selected as a member of the Boston Business Journal's Top 40 Under 40 class for 2010.

Curtis is the author of three books, *Mind The Gap: Getting Business Results in Multigenerational Organizations*, *Generation X Approved: Top 20 Keys to Effective Leadership*, as well as the wildly successful *Stuck in the Middle: A Generation X View of Talent Management*.

As a published author, Curtis has been a go-to expert on the subject of talent management, having been featured in/on CNNMoney.com's "Ask Annie" column, Wall Street Journal's FINS blog, Ebony.com, Huffington Post and a number of other regional and national outlets.

For more information on Dr. Curtis L. Odom as an author, speaker, facilitator, consultant, and executive coach, visit www.doctorcurtisodom.com